AN ARAMAIC HANDB

PORTA LINGUARUM ORIENTALIUM
HERAUSGEGEBEN VON BERTHOLD SPULER UND HANS WEHR

NEUE SERIE

X

AN ARAMAIC HANDBOOK

1967

OTTO HARRASSOWITZ · WIESBADEN

AN ARAMAIC HANDBOOK

WITH CONTRIBUTIONS BY

Z. BEN-HAYYIM
M. BLACK
A. DUPONT-SOMMER
H. L. GINSBERG
H. INGHOLT
R. KÖBERT
E. Y. KUTSCHER
R. MACUCH
H. J. POLOTSKY
H. RITTER
F. ROSENTHAL
A. SPITALER

EDITED BY

FRANZ ROSENTHAL

PART I/2

GLOSSARY

1967

OTTO HARRASSOWITZ · WIESBADEN

Satz und Druck:
Buchdruckerei J. J. Augustin, Glückstadt
Hoppenstedt · Hessische Druckerei GmbH., Darmstadt
Buchdruckerei Hubert & Co., Göttingen
Gesamtherstellung: Hubert & Co., Göttingen
Printed in Germany

Table of Contents

Part I/2

	Part I/2 Glossary page	Part I/1 Texts page
I. Ancient Aramaic Monumental Inscriptions (Dupont-Sommer)	1	1
II. Aramaic Texts from Achaemenid Times (Rosenthal)	8	10
III. Biblical Aramaic (Ginsberg)	16	17
IV. Palmyrene-Hatran-Nabataean (Ingholt)	42	40
V. Jewish Palestinian Aramaic (Kutscher)	52	51

Table of Contents

Part II

VI. Samaritan (Ben-Hayyim)
VII. Palestinian Syriac (Black)
VIII. Syriac (Köbert)
IX. Babylonian Talmudic (Kutscher)
X. Mandaic (Macuch)
XI. The Aramaic Dialect of Ma'lūla (Spitaler)
XII. Eastern Neo-Aramaic: Urmi and Zakho (Polotsky)
XIII. Ṭūrōyo (Ṭōrānī) (Ritter)

The Glossaries

(All the glossaries, except those for the modern dialects, follow the ordinary sequence of the Semitic [Hebrew] alphabet [with slight modifications in the case of Mandaic], regardless of whether Aramaic characters or a Latin transliteration is used. The sequence adopted in connection with the modern dialects is basically that of the Latin alphabet; the necessary modifications are indicated in the alphabets appearing at the head of each of the glossaries in question.)

I. ANCIENT ARAMAIC MONUMENTAL INSCRIPTIONS

(André Dupont-Sommer) *

(Roots or words that occur only in completely restored passages are enclosed in square brackets.)

ʾ

ʾb father, suff. *ʾby*, *ʾb(w)h*, pl. suff. *ʾbhy*.
ʾbd to perish; *hap.* to cause to perish.
ʾbh *tn*-reflexive (cf. Akk.) *htnʾbw* to be envious.
[*ʾbn* stone.]
ʾbn Ibni (proper name) (Pan. 7?).
ʾgbr Agbar (proper name).
ʾdm (place name, I Sfire A 10, 35).
ʾw or.
ʾz then.
ʾḥ brother, suff. *ʾḥk*, pl. cstr. (accus.) *ʾḥy*, suff. *ʾḥy*, *ʾḥwh*. Cf. also *ʾyḥ*.
ʾḥw vegetation, suff. *ʾḥwh*.
ʾḥz to take, to seize (*b* something); *hitp.* to be closed (*mn* to), with negation *lʾtʾḥz*.
ʾḥrh posterity, suff. *ʾḥrth*; *ʾḥrh*, *lʾḥrh* thereafter; *ʾḥrn* other.
ʾyh see *ʾyt*.
ʾyḥ brother, relative, pl. cstr. *ʾyḥy*, suff. *ʾyḥh*.
ʾyk zy, *ʾykh zy* like as (conj.).
ʾyt prep. introducing the direct object (accus.), suff. *ʾyty*, *ʾy⟨t⟩h*.
ʾkl to eat, to devour; *ʾkl* (part.) devourer.
ʾl (prep.) to, suff. *ʾly*, *ʾlwh*.
ʾl not (used for prohibitions).
ʾl these.
ʾl El (deity).
ʾlh god, pl. *ʾlhn*, (accus.) *ʾlhy*, cstr. *ʾlhy*, det. *ʾlhyʾ*.
ʾlh curse, conspiracy (Pan. 2?).
ʾlwr Ilu-Wēr (or Ilu-Mēr, one of the names of the god Hadad),
ʾln these.
ʾmn firmly (Pan. 21).
ʾmr to say, to speak about.
ʾmr lamb.
ʾnh I.
ʾnht Anahita (f. deity).
ʾnky I (perhaps archaic Aramaic, or a loan from Canaanite).
**ʾnp* (dual) face, surface, suff. *ʾpy*, *ʾpwh*, *ʾpyh*. Cf. *rwḥ*.
ʾnš mankind, *br ʾnš* man, human being.

---

* The author wishes to thank Dr. Maurice Sznycer for his help in preparing the manuscript of the texts and in establishing the glossary on the basis of the author's readings, translations, and notes.

**ʾnt* see *ʾt*.
ʾsnb (Pan. 6?).
ʾsr to fetter, to imprison (imp. suff. *ʾsrh* III Sfire 18).
ʾp further.
ʾp see *ʾnp*.
ʾpš Afis(?, place name).
ʾṣr treasure, treasury.
[*ʾr*] Irra (deity).
ʾrbh locust.
ʾrḥ (f.) road.
ʾrk *hap.* to lengthen.
ʾrm Aram (country).
ʾrnb hare.
ʾrnh (place name).
ʾrpd Arpad (town).
ʾrṣh couch, sarcophagus, det. *ʾrṣtʾ*, suff. *ʾrṣty*, *ʾrṣth*.
ʾrq earth, land, territory, suff. *ʾrqy*, *ʾrqk*, *ʾrqh*.
ʾrrṭw Urartu (reading uncertain, cf. *brgʾyh*).
ʾš man, det *ʾšʾ*.
ʾš fire.
ʾšh woman, pl. (accus.) *nšy*, cstr. *nšy*.
ʾšm (= *šm*) name.
ʾšr place, trace, *ʾšr ydy* my achievements, suff. *ʾšrk*, *ʾšrh*, *ʾšrkm*; *bʾšr* in the place of, suff. *bʾšry*, *bʾšrh* (but III Sfire 7: to his place).
ʾšr, *ʾšwr* Assur, Assyria.
ʾt you (sg. m.).
ʾth to come.

B

b in (local), through (instrumental), on (day, road), upon, at (wheel, feet), because of. Cf. also *yd*.
bʾš *hap.* to make miserable.
by, *byt* house, temple, palace, suff. *byty*, *byth*, pl. cstr. *bty*.
**byn* see *bny*.
bynn (place name?).
bytʾl Bethel (place name?).
bkh to mourn (perf. 3. f. sg. with suff. *bkyth*, 3. pl. m. with suff. *bkwny*, *bkyh*).
bkth hen.
bny among (III Sfire 21), suff. *bnyhm*.
bnh to build.
bnt see *br*.
bʿh to seek, to ask for.
bʿl lord, owner, inhabitant, pl. (accus.) *bʿly*, cstr. *bʿly*, suff. *bʿlyh*— *bʿl* Baʿal (deity), *bʿl ʿynn* Baʿal of springs(?); *bʿlšmyn* Baʿal-Šamayn (deity).
br son, suff. *bry*, *brk*, *brh*, pl. cstr. *bny*, suff. *bny*, *bnwh*; f. pl. *bnt* daughters [dependencies I Sfire A 35]. Cf. also *ʾnš*.
brgʾyh Bar-gaʾayah (lit. "son of majesty" = *magnificus*, *augustus*, an honorific title taking the place of the ruler's proper name in official usage), possibly referring to Sardur III, king of Urartu.
brgš Bar-Guš (proper name), referring to the king of Bīt Agushi, located adjacent to Laʿaš, with the capital city of Arpad. Cf. also *gš*.
brd hail.
brhdd Bar-Hadad (proper name).
brṣr Bar-Ṣur (proper name).
brrkb, *brkb* Bar-Rekub (proper name).

G

gbl territory, suff. *gbly*, *gblh*.
gbr man; [f. cstr. *gbrt* woman].
gw *bgw* within, suff. *bgwh* in its midst.
gzr to cut up, to conclude (treaty, cf. H. *krt bryt*, Greek *ὅρκια τέμνειν*).
glgl wheel.
gm also, furthermore.
gnb bandit(?)
grgm Gurgum (country).
gš Guš. See *brgš*.

D

dbrh (written by mistake *dbhh*) wasp.
dm blood, suff. *dmy*.
dmšq Damascus.
[*dnny* Danuna (country)?]
[*drwm* south?]

H

hʾ (*hw* Sfire 22?) he; *hʾ* she; *hʾ* that (demonstrative pronoun, m. and f.).
hdd Hadad (deity).

hwh to be, to become, to belong (perf. 3. sg. f. *hwt*, but Pan. 5: *hwyt*).
hwm to lament (inf. abs. *hwm*); *hitp.* to lament (*ʾthmw*).
hlk to go (impf. *ʾhk*, *yhkn*, f. *yhkn*).
hm (suff. 3. pl. m.).
hmw they (m.).
hmwn tumult.
hml upheaval, crash.
hn if, *hn lhn* (in III Sfire) if (you do) not (do) so.
hn they (f.)
hns to remove (impf. *thns* (Nerab b 8), impf. suff. *yhnsnh*, *thnsny*, impf. pass. *thns*).
hpk to overturn.
hrg to kill.
hrh to become pregnant.

W

w and, introducing an apodosis, used as *wâw* conversive; *wʾ* Pan. 5.

Z

zʾ this (f.), this matter.
zhb gold.
zḥl to fear.
zy relative pronoun, conj. (so that, because); *zy ly* mine, *zy lk* yours. Cf. also *ʾyk*, *kl*.
zkr memorial; *zkr* Zakir (proper name); *zkrn* remembrance, memorandum.
zlh cheap, sg. cstr. (or pl. abs. f.) *zlt*.
zn, *znh* this (m.).
zrʿ to sow; *zrʿ* seed, progeny, suff. *zrʿk*.
zrpnt Zarpanit (f. deity).

Ḥ

ḥbz to hit (= *ḥbṭ* found in various Semitic languages).
ḥbr association, community, state (I Sfire A 4).
ḥd one, cstr. *ḥd* (or *ḥd mn*) one of, suff. *ḥdhm*.
ḥwg *mḥgt* district.
ḥwh snake.
ḥzʾl Hazael (proper name).
ḥzh to see (part. *mḥzh* = *mh ḥzh*; inf. *lḥzyh*); *hitp.* to appear (impf. with negation *lytḥzh*); pl. *ḥzyn* seers.
ḥzz (place name, Ḥazaz?).
ḥzrk Ḥazrek, Hadrach (place name).
ḥṭh wheat.
ḥyn (pl.) life.
ḥkmh wisdom, suff. *ḥkmth*.
ḥlb Aleppo, *hdd ḥlb* Hadad of Aleppo.
ḥll to pierce, to kill, *ḥly* those killed (accus.) (?).
ḥlm dream.
ḥlp *pa.* (*hap.*?) to replace (jussive suff. *yḥlph*?).
ḥmt Ḥamath (country).
ḥnʾ *pa.* to place (perf. suff. *ḥnʾh* Pan. 12?).
ḥnh *mḥnh* army, cstr. *mḥnt*, suff. *mḥnth*, pl. *mḥnt*, suff. *mḥnwthm*.
ḥsn fortification.
ḥpṣ wish, suff. *ḥpṣy*.
ḥṣ arrow.
ḥṣl to deliver (< *ḥlṣ*, or *leg.* *ʾhṣlk*, from the root *nṣl*?).
ḥṣr grass.
ḥrb (f.) sword.
ḥrb ruined, pl. f. *ḥrbt*.
ḥrṣ trench, moat.
ḥšb *nipʿal* (*nḥšb*) to be esteemed, counted (Pan. 10?).

Ṭ

ṭb good, f. good condition, good deeds (things), cstr. *ṭbt*, det. *ṭbtʾ*. Cf. also *yṭb*.

Y

yʾdy Yaʾudi (country).
ybl to bring.
ybl ram (Pan. 21?).
yd hand, suff. *ydy*, *ydh*, pl. suff. *ydy*, [*ydwh*], *byd* (prep.) through.
ydd *mwdd* friend, pl. suff. *mwddwh*.
ywm day, pl. cstr. *ywmy*, suff. *ywmy*, (gen./accus.) *ywmyh*.
yḥd *hap.* to unite (perf. *hwḥd*).
yṭb hap. to cause to prosper (with suff. *hyṭbh*, *hyṭbth*).
yllh lamentation.
ynq *hap.* to nurse (jussive 3. pl. f. *yhynqn*); part. f. wet nurse, pl. *mhynqn*.
ysp *hap.* to add (perf. *hwspt*).

yqʾ *hap.* to bring out (impf. *ywqʾ* Pan. 21?); *mwqʾ* (sun)rise, east.
yqd to burn (intrans.) (impf. *yqd*, *tqd*).
yrq verdure.
yrt to inherit (jussive *yrt*).
yšb to sit, to stay, to reside (impf. *yšb*, *yšbn*, imp. *šbw*), part. pass. pl. f. *yšbt* inhabited; *hap.* to settle, to instal (perf. *hwšbt*, suff. *hwšbny*); *mšb* throne, suff. *mšbh*.
yšmn desert.
ytr rest, remainder, suff. *ytrh*.

K

k (prep.) like as. Cf. also *kzy*, *kʿt*.
[*kbd* *pa.* to honor.]
kbr to abound; *hap.* to make numerous; *kbr* might.
kdʾh Kadiʾah (f. deity).
kh thus.
kzy when.
kṭl see *qtl*.
ky for (particle).
kym likewise.
kyṣ summer, *byt kyṣʾ* summer palace.
kl all, entire, every, everything, everybody, (followed by negation) any, suff. *klh*; *klmh* every, every kind of, *bklmh zy* whenever.
klmw Kilamū (proper name).
kmr priest.
kn so, thus.
knp fringe.
knr cithara.
ksp silver.
kʿt now.
kpyr vessel, ship (Pan. 10: pl. gen. *kpyry*?).
kpr village, pl. suff. *kpryh*.
krsʾ throne, suff. *krsʾy* (miswritten *khsʾy*).
ktb to write.
ktk KTK (Bar-gaʾayah's capital or realm, as yet unexplained, cf. *brgʾyh*).

L

l to, for (direction, purpose, possession, dative, preceding inf.), because of. Cf. also *zy*.
l not.
lʾk see *mlʾk*.
lbb heart, suff. *lbbk*.
lbš clothes, suff. *lbšy*.
lgr see *rgl*.
ldd see *lwd*.
lhn see *hn*.
lw certainly.
lwd (*ldd*?) *hap.* to efface (impf. *ʾhld*).
lḥh bad, pl. f. *lḥyt* (note *-ât*, for later *-ân*); *lḥyh* evil (noun), pl. *lḥyt*.
lḥm food, victuals.
lylh night.
lyš there is not, suff. *lyšh*.
lʿš Laʿaš (country).
lṣ Laṣ (f. deity).
lqḥ to take, to perceive (words) (impf. *tqḥ*, impf. pass. *yqḥn*); *lqḥ* conqueror (I Sfire A 29—30?).
lšn tongue, suff. *lšnk*.

M

m see *mh*.
mʾn vessel, object.
mblh (place name?).
mdrʾ (place name?).
mh, *m* what?, that which, whatever. Cf. also *kl*.
mwdd see *ydd*.
mwkr price, expensive thing, pl. (nom.) *mwkrw* (?).
mwqʾ see *yqʾ*.
mwt to die (perf. *mt*, *mtt*, impf. *ymwt*); *hap.* to kill (impf./jussive suff. *ymth*, inf. *lhmtt*, suff. *lhmtty*); *mwt* death; *mmth* death, suff. *mmtth*.
mzh (place name?).
mḥʾ to beat, to erect (rampart), to lay (siege).
mḥgt see *ḥwg*.
mḥzh = *mh ḥzh*.
mḥnh see *ḥnh*.
mk see *mn*.
mlʾ *pa.* to fill (Pan. 4).
mlʾk ambassador, suff. *mlʾky*, *mlʾkh*.
mlh see *mll*.
mlz Meliz (Malatya) (country).
mlḥ salt.
mlk to rule; *pa.* to make (someone) king (perf. suff. *mlkh* Pan. 7); *hap.* to make (someone) king (perf. suff. *hmlkny*, *hmlktk*); *mlk* king, suff. *mlky*, *mlkh*, pl. *mlkn*,

(nom.) *mlkw*, (gen./accus.) *mlky*, cstr. *mlky*, det. *mlkyʾ*; *mlk(w)t* kingdom, realm, suff. *mlkty*, *mlkth*.
mll *pa.* to speak; *mlh* word, pl. *mln*, cstr. *mly*, det. *mlyʾ*, suff. *mlwh*.
mlš (deity).
mmth see *mwt*.
mn from (local, partitive "some", "some of", see also *ḥd*), (more, higher, deeper, more numerous) than, suff. *mny*, *mk* (2. sg. m.).
mn whoever.
msgrh see *sgr*.
mʿyn see *ʿyn*.
mʿn in *lmʿn* so that, (followed by negation) lest.
mʿrb see *ʿrb*.
mṣʿh midst, cstr. *mṣʿt*.
mṣr see *ṣrr*.
mṣr Muṣru (country).
mrʾ lord, master, suff. *mrʾy*, *mrʾh*, *mrʾkm*.
mrbh (place name?).
mrdk Marduk (deity).
mrmh perfidy, pl. *mrmt*.
mrq (part.) destroyer.
mśky relief, stela (cf. H.).
mšb see *yšb*.
mšwh smoke, pl. *mšwt* (Pan. 21?).
mšḥ to anoint; *mšḥ* oil.
mšl to exercise command (*b* over).
mt certainly.
mtʿʾl Matiʿel (proper name).

N

nbʾ Nebo (deity).
nbš soul, suff. *nbšh*, *nbšhm*.
ngʿ *hap.* to remove (impf. *yhgʿ*).
ngr prefect, suff. *ngry*.
nḥš bronze.
nḥšb see *ḥšb*.
nkh blow.
nkl Nikkal (f. deity).
nkr Nakar (deity).
nmrh panther.
nsḥ to tear out (impf./jussive *ysḥw*).
nsk to pour out, to hand out (impf. *ysk*, *tsk*).
[*npl* to fall (impf. *ypln*).]
npq to come out (impf. *ypq*).
nṣb stela.
nṣr to guard (impf. *tnṣr*, *lyṣr*, jussive *yṣrw*, impf. pass. *ynṣr*).
nqm to avenge (impf. *yqm*, *tqm*).
nr Ner (deity).
nrb Nerab (place name).
nrgl Nergal (deity).
nśʾ to lift, to bring up, to take away (impf. *yśʾ*, *tśʾ*, *ʾśʾ*).
nšk Nušku (deity).
nšn, *nšy* see *ʾšh*.

S

sbt Sibitti (deity).
sgr *msgrh* prison, pl. *msgrt*.
sḥrh entourage, suff. *sḥrty*.
skr *hap.* to hand over (impf. *yhskr*, *yskr*, *yhskrn*, suff. *thskrhm*, inf. abs. *hskr*).
slq to come up, to rise (impf. *ysq*, *ysqn*).
smk to lean (trans.)
ss moth (*tinea*).
ssyh mare.
spr inscription.
srs eunuch.

ʿ

ʿbd to do, to serve, to commit (perfidy); [*hitp.* to be done]; *ʿbd* servant, pl. suff. *ʿbdy*.
ʿbr to forgive (impf. *ʾʿbr*); *hap.* to transfer, to cause (someone) to disappear (impf. suff. *yʿbrnh*).
ʿgl calf.
ʿd, *wʿd* (prep.) until, unto; *ʿd* (conj.) until.
ʿdd prophet, pl. *ʿddn*.
**ʿdn* (pl.) treaty, pact, cstr. *ʿdy*, det. *ʿdyʾ* (probably, < *w/yʿd* "to fix," cf. Akk. *wadū*, *adū*, Syr. *waʿdā*).
ʿwr *hap.* to blind (impf. pass. *yʿr*).
ʿyl *ʿl* foal.
ʿyn eye, pl. suff. *ʿyny*, *ʿynykm*; *mʿyn* spring, pl. *mʿynn*. See also *bʿl*.
ʿl upon, over, against, at, suff. *ʿly*, *ʿlyk*, *ʿlh*, *ʿlyh*.
ʿl see *ʿyl*.
ʿly ʾrm Upper Aram; *ʿlyh* upper part, suff. *ʿlyth*; *ʿlyn* Elyōn (deity).
[*ʿlylwt* action, behavior.]
ʿlym child.
ʿll to enter (part. *ʿll*).
ʿlm eternity.
ʿm with, suff. *ʿmy*, *ʿmk*.

ʿm people, suff. *ʿmy*, *ʿmh*, pl. det. *ʿmyʾ*(?).
ʿml to work hard.
ʿml affliction.
ʿmq *hap.* to dig.
ʿmq ʿAmq (country).
ʿnh to answer, to hear (impf. suff. *yʿnny*).
ʿnh humble.
ʿqh magpie(?).
ʿqr progeny, suff. *ʿqry*, *ʿqrk*, *ʿqrh*.
ʿqrb scorpion.
ʿrb *mʿrb* sunset, west.
ʿśq to wrong (impf. *tʿśq*, suff. *tʿśqny*).
ʿśr ten.
ʿtrsmk ʿAtarsamak (proper name).

P

p (*pʾ*, *py*) and.
pḥh governor, pl. cstr. (accus.) *pḥy*.
plṭ to save (perf. suff. *plṭwh*).
pm mouth, suff. *pmy*.
pnh to return (intrans.) (jussive *tpnw*).
pnmw Panamû (proper name).
pqd official, pl. suff. *pqdy*.
pqḥ to open (imp. *pqḥw*).
prs half (measure?).
prš horseman, horsemen.
pšš to enlarge.
ptḥ to open (part. pass. f. *ptḥh*).

Ṣ

ṣby gazelle.
ṣdh owl.
ṣdq loyalty, suff. *ṣdqy*, *ṣdqh*; *ṣdqh* righteousness, suff. *ṣdqty*.
ṣwlh abyss.
[*ṣy* desert animal.]
ṣlm picture, suff. *ṣlmh*.
[*ṣpwn* north(?).]
ṣrr *mṣr* siege.

Q

qbr grave.
qdm (prep.) before (local), suff. *qdmwh*; *qdmh* former condition, suff. *qdmth*.
qwh Que (Cilicia).
qwm to stand, to arise, to cost (*b* so-and-so much); *hap.* to erect.
qyrh town, pl. *qyrt* (Pan. 4, 15). See also *qryh*.
ql sound, voice.
qml vermin.
qnwʾl (proper name).
qqbtn partridge(?).
[*qrʾ* to call (perf. suff. *qrʾny*).]
qryh town. See also *qyrh*.
qrl (proper name).
qrq to flee; *qrq* (part.) fugitive, suff. *qrqy*, *qrqhm*.
qšt bow.
qtl to kill (impf. *yqtl*, *yqtln*, jussive with suff. *ykṭlwk*, imp. *qtl*, *qtlw*, part. pass. pl. f. *qtylt*).

R

rʾš head, suff. *rʾšy*.
rb great, (pl.) many, pl. f. *rbt*, pl. m. *rbrbn*; (pl.) magnates, suff. *rbwh*.
[*rbh* to become great.]
rbʿ fourth generation; (pl.) the four quarters (of the earth), cstr. m. *rbʿy*, f. *rbʿt*.
[*rbq* lair.]
rgl (*lgr*) foot, pl. cstr. *lgry*.
rwḥ spirit, *rwḥ ʾpwh* his life.
rwm *hap.* to raise, to take away (perf. *hrmw*, impf. *thrm*).
rwṣ to run (perf. *rṣt*).
rḥbh Raḥbah (place name).
rḥmn (pl.) affection, suff. *rḥmh*.
ryb to be in conflict (impf. *yrb*).
rkb chariot, charioteers.
rkbʾl Rekub-El (deity, protector of the dynasty of Śamʾal).
rmh see *mrmh*.
rph *hap.* to release (perf. *hrpy*).
rqh to be conciliatory (impf. *trqh*, inf. *rqh*: III Sfire 18—19).
rqq to capture (impf. suff. *trqhm*, *ʾrqhm*, imp. *rqw*, inf. *rqh*: III Sfire 6).
ršh to protest (impf. with negation *ltršh*).

Ś

śʾh ewe, *śʾt* (I Sfire A 21), pl. *śʾn*.
śbʿ to be sated.
śgb (pl.) magnates, suff. *śgbwh*.
śhd witness, pl. *śhdn*.
śhr Śahar (deity).
śym to set up, to place, to make, to lay (siege), to change (*b* to), to

give (someone a name), to appoint (perf. *śm, śmt, śmw,* suff. *śmny, śmth, śmwny,* impf. *ʾśm, tśmw,* jussive *yśmw*).

śmʾl Śamʾal (country).

śnʾ enemy, pl. suff. *śnʾy, śnʾwh.*

śʿrh barley.

śph lip, dual suff. *śptyk, śptwh.*

śrgwn Sargon (proper name) (?).

śtw winter, *byt śtwʾ* winter palace.

Š

š belonging to (Nerab a 1 and b 1).

šʾl to demand.

šby captives.

šbʿ seven, cstr. *šbʿt*; *šbʿy* seventy.

šbr to break (impf. *yšbr,* pass. *tšbr*).

[*šd* breast, pl. suff. *šdyhn.*]

šwb to return, to be restored to (perf. *šbt*); *hap.* to return (trans.), (+ *šybt*) to restore (perf. *hšb, hšbw,* impf. *ʾhšb,* suff. *thšbhm*); *šybh* restoration, cstr. *šybt.*

šwṭ to rove, *bšṭ* in search of.

šwr see *šr.*

šwrh cow.

šḥd to give presents to.

šḥṭ *hitpa.* to be ravaged (< *šḥt,* cf. Syr.).

šḥlyn water cress (?).

šḥt criminal (?); *šḥth* extermination (?).

šṭrb (Panamū 6?).

šybh see *šwb.*

šlh to stay quiet (imp. pl. *šlw*).

šlḥ to send, to send forth, to send (a message) (inf. [*pa.*?] *lšlḥ* III Sfire 8).

šm name, suff. *šmk.* See also *ʾšm.*

šm there.

šmyn heaven.

šmʿ *hitp.* to be heard (impf. *ytšmʿ*).

šmrg (Panamū 16?).

šmš sun, Šamaš (deity) (*šmšʾ*, in I Sfire C 5, Šamaš as the god of justice, or perhaps, king Bargaʾayah himself called "The Sun," as, for instance, the Hittite kings?).

šnh year, cstr. *šnt,* pl. *šnn.*

šnzrbn Sin-zir-ibni (proper name).

šʿwtʾ wax.

šʿl fox, jackal.

špr beautiful.

šql shekel.

šqr to betray (*l* someone, but always *bʿdyʾ* the treaty).

šr, šwr rampart.

šrh to release (impf./jussive suff. *tšryh*).

šrn wild cat.

šrn (place name?).

šrš root, lineage, suff. *šršh.*

šš six, *ššt ʿśr* sixteen.

šth to drink (perf. *štt,* [impf. *tšty*]).

T

tgltpl(y)sr Tiglath-pileser (proper name).

twʾm (place name).

twy (meaning uncertain, perhaps, the name of a river causing a calamitous inundation).

twlʿh worm, maggot.

tḥt (prep.) underneath, *ltḥtkm* where you are; *tḥt* lower end, suff. *tḥth* (lower Aram); *tḥtyh* lower part, suff. *tḥtyth.*

tl tell, hill of ruins.

tlʾym (f.) (place name).

tpp to strike (imp. suff. *tph, tpwh*).

tšmt Tašmet (f. deity).

II. ARAMAIC TEXTS FROM ACHAEMENID TIMES

(Franz Rosenthal)

(Unless otherwise specified, proper names, recognizable by the use of capitals, are male proper names.)

ʾ

ʾ abbreviation of *ʾšl* cord (measure) (Akk. *ašlu*), or of *ʾrdb ardabb* (the area being measured on the basis of the amount of seed required, cf. *The Assyrian Dictionary, s.v. zēru*).

ʾb father, pl. *ʾbhn*.

ʾbd to perish, to be lost (get spoiled ?).

ʾbh (proper name of uncertain origin [Aram. Abbā ?]).

ʾbn stone, *ʾbny mlkʾ* royal weight.

ʾbšwk prob. newcomer not belonging to the regular labor force, or deserter (P.).

ʾgwr temple (Akk. *ekurru*).

ʾgrh, ʾgrt letter (Akk. *egirtu*).

ʾdyn then.

ʾw or.

ʾwsry Osiris (Eg. deity).

ʾwstn Ustāna, Ostanes (P.).

ʾwryh Ūrīyāh (H.).

ʾzl to go.

ʾḥ brother; *ʾḥh* sister.

ʾḥd (*ʾḥz*) to take.

ʾḥyw Aḥyō (H.).

ʾḥyqr Aḥiqar (Akk. *a-ḫu-ʾu-qa-a-ri*, cf. J. van Dijk, in *XVIII. vorläufiger Bericht . . . Ausgrabungen in Uruk-Warka* [1962], 45).

ʾḥr after (prep., temporal and local), then; *ʿl ʾḥrn* eventually; *ʾḥrn* other.

ʾyš someone.

ʾytw (proper name of uncertain reading [H. *ʾytn* ?]).

ʾyty there is.

ʾl not (used for prohibitions).

ʾl to (addressee of a letter).

ʾlh God.

ʾlh these.

ʾlk those.

ʾlp *hitpa.* to be taught; *ʾlpn* discipline.

ʾlp thousand.

ʾlp boat.

ʾm mother.

ʾmh female slave.

ʾmh cubit, pl. *ʾmn*.

ʾmwn Amōn (Eg. ?), or rather (Anatolian) Ammuwana (cf. A. Goetze, in *Journal of Cuneiform Studies*, XVI [1962], 54—57).

ʾmr to say, to speak, *lʾmr, lmmr* to say, as follows; *ʾmr* utterance. See also *krṣ*.

ʾnb fruit

ʾndrw (proper name of uncertain [P. ?] origin).

ʾnh I.

ʾnḥnh we.

ʾnp (pl. *ʾnpn, ʾpn*) face.

ʾnt you (sg. m.).

ʾnth woman, wife, pl. *nšn* (before a woman's name, a polite form of address ?); *ʾntw* wifehood, marriage.

ʾnty you (sg. f.).

ʾntm you (pl. m.).

ʾsmrwp (proper name prob. of Anatolian origin).

ʾspmt (Eg. proper name).

ʾsrḥʾdn Aššur-aḫ-iddin, Esarhaddon (Akk.).

ʾp also, further.

ʾp see *ʾnp*.

ʾpw also.

ʾpm still (again ?).

ʾrbʿ four.

ʾrwstmr (P. [?] proper name).

ʾrz cedar.

ʾrḥ half brick (or something like "fetter") (Akk. *arḫu?*).
ʾryyšʾ (P.[?] proper name).
ʾrk length; *ʾryk* long.
ʾrmy Aramaean.
ʾrmlh widow.
ʾrʿ (*ʾrq*) earth, ground, plot of land.
ʾršm Aršāma, Arsames (P.).
ʾrtbnw Artabānū (P.).
ʾrthnt Artahant (P.).
ʾrtwhy Artōhī (P.).
ʾrtḥšsš Artaḫšaśa, Artaxerxes (P.).
ʾšh fire.
ʾšrn materials, furnishings (P.).
ʾth to come, to go; *hap̄*. *hyty* to bring.
ʾtwr Assyria.
ʾtr place, station.
ʾtrwprn (P. proper name, with the last element being *farna*).

B

b in (local and temporal), on (temporal and local), at (temporal), upon, by (oath). See also *bzy*, *gw*, *znh*, *yd*, *šm*.
(*bʾš*) *bʾyš* bad, evil, (f.) evil (noun).
bb gate.
bbly Babylonian.
bg domain (P.).
bgwhy Bāgōhī, Bagoas (P.).
bgsrw Bāgasarū (P.).
bgprn Bāgafarna (P.).
bdykr prob. maker of jewelry, artist (P.).
bzy since, because (conj.).
bzʿ to tear.
by see *byt*.
byn between, among, in.
byrh citadel, fortified town.
byt house, estate, establishment, abs. *by*, *byt zrʿ* field (area), *byt mdbḥʾ* temple. Cf. also *br*.
blh (det. *bltʾ*) load (Akk. *biltu*).
bnh to build, to rebuild; *hitp*. to be built, rebuilt; *bnyn* construction.
bny-, *bnn* see *br*.
bʿh to wish, to seek.
bʿl master, owner, husband, inhabitant, recipient, giver (of counsel).
bqṭ see *qṭ*.
bql vegetables, rather than "malt" (Akk. *buqlu*).
br son, pl. *bnn*, *bny-*, *br bytʾ* prince (loan trans. of P. *vispuhr*); *brh* daughter.
(*brr*) *br mn zy* except if.
(*brk*) *bryk* blessed.
brq lightning.
bśm scented.
bśr flesh.
bšm see *šm*.

G

gbr man.
gdwl Gaḏōl; *gdlyh* Gᵉḏalyāh (H.).
(*gw*) *bgw* within, on the recto(?), in this connection.
gld skin.
gmryh Gᵉmaryāh (H.).
grd workmen's gang (P. *gard*).
grh to bring (suit) (Akk. *gerū*).

D

dbb complaint (Akk. *dabābu*).
dbḥ (*zbḥ*) sacrifice; *mdbḥ* altar. See also *byt*.
dbq to be attached, adjacent.
dbr to lead. See also *ʿl*.
dgl detachment (of soldiers).
dhb (*zhb*) gold.
dḥl to be afraid.
dyn (*dīn*) suit, court; (*dayyān*) judge.
dkr (*zkr*) to remember; *zkrn* memorandum.
dlyh Dᵉlāyāh (H.).
dm blood.
dmydt Dāmīdāta (P.).
dmn (pl.) value.
dnh valid document (Akk. *dannatu*) (rather than = *znh*, in B 3, endorsement).
drgmn Dargmana (P.).
drywhwš, *dryhwš* Dārayavahūš, Darius (P.).
dš leaf of a door, pl. *dšn*, *dššn*.

H

hʾ behold!
hddnwry Hadadnūrī.
hw he, that is (i. e.).
hwh to be.
hwk to go, to pass away. Cf. Biblical Aramaic *hlk*.
hwmdt Hawmadāta (P.).

hwšʿ Hōšeʿ, Hosea (H.).
hy she.
hykl palace.
hyll see *yll*.
hyty see *ʾth*.
hlk see *hwk*; *hlk* taxes (Akk. *ilku*).
hmw they, them.
hmwnyt in concert (with) (P.).
hmrkr accountant (P. *hamārakara*).
hn if. See also *lʾ*, *lhn*, *lw*, *lmh*.
hndyz mustered (soldiers) (P. *handēz*).
hnʿl see *ʿll*.

W

w and, (introducing a subordinate clause) while, (A 1²⁷) introducing apodosis, *wlʾ* without (prep.).
wydrng (P. proper name [Vīdranga?]).
wryzt Varyazāta (P.).
wršbr farm expert (?) (P.).

Z

zʾ this (f.).
zbḥ see *dbḥ*.
zhb see *dhb*.
zwn portion (?) (P.?).
zy relative pronoun, genitive particle, made of (a certain material), whoever. Cf. also *bzy*, *brr*, *zyl-*, *kzy*, *mh*, *mn*, *ʿd*, *ʿl*.
zyl- independent possessive pronoun.
zyn see *zn*.
zk that (m. and f. demonstrative pronoun).
zkwr Zakkūr (H.).
zky that (m. demonstrative pronoun).
zky innocent.
zkr, *zkrn* see *dkr*.
zkryh Zᵉḵaryāh (H.).
zn (*zyn*) weapon (P., Avestan *zaēna*).
znh this (m.), *bznh* here, *kznh* thus.
znk that (m. demonstrative pronoun).
(*zʿr*) *zʿyr* terrifying (Ar. *ḏʿr*?).
zʿrrh meddlar.
zpt see *yzp*.
zrʿ seed. See also *byt*.
(*zrq*) *mzrq* basin.

Ḥ

ḥbl *pa.* to harm.
ḥd, f. *ḥdh* one, a . . ., *ḥd kḥd* both alike.
(*ḥdy*) *ḥdh* glad.
ḥdt new.
ḥwh *pa*, *hap̄*. to inform, to show, — *b* to let one have his revenge on.
ḥwṭ thread (?), see *ḥm*.
ḥzh to see, — *b* to find oneself revenged on; *mḥzy* mirror.
ḥṭ cash (Akk. *ḫāṭu*).
ḥṭʾ sin, offense.
ḥṭr rod.
ḥyh to live; *hap̄*. to keep alive, to let live; *ḥyn* life, *ḥylyhh* by the life of Yᵉhō.
ḥyl military force, troop, army, power. See also *rb*.
ḥylyhh see *ḥyh*.
ḥylky Cilician.
ḥkm *pa.* to teach; *ḥkym* wise; *ḥkmh* wisdom.
ḥlp to succeed (trans.); *hap̄*. to send in return; *ḥlp* instead of.
ḥlr one-tenth of a shekel (Akk. *ḫallūru*).
ḥm bit of straw (Akk. *ḫāmu*), *mn ḥm ʿd ḥwṭ* altogether, everything.
ḥmr to be angry (*ʿl* with); *ḥmr lbbh* anger (?).
ḥmr wine.
ḥmr donkey.
ḥnwb Ḫnūb (Eg. deity).
ḥnzny (proper name of uncertain reading).
ḥs bitter lettuce, pl. *ḥsyn*.
ḥsh saint, pl. det. *ḥsyh*.
ḥsn *hap̄*. to possess, to take possession of, to keep in possession, *mḥḥsn* property owner; *ḥsyn* strong.
ḥpn handful.
ḥrzmy Ḫvārezmian.
(*ḥrr*) *ḥr* nobleman.
ḥršyn (P. proper name).
(*ḥšb*) *ḥšbn* bill.
ḥšk *hap̄*. to withhold.
ḥšl to pay (taxes).

Ṭ

ṭb good, (pl. f.) goodness, good deeds. Cf. also *yṭb*.
ṭbh (*ṭby*) gazelle.
ṭwr mountain.
(*ṭll*) *mṭll* roof.

ṭʿm to taste, to eat; *ṭʿm* order.
ṭʿn to impose (an oath).

Y

yb Yeb (Elephantine, Eg. place name).
ybl to bring.
ygdl Yiḡdal (H.).
yd hand, *byd* through.
ydnyh (H. proper name [Yᵉḏonyāh?]).
ydʿ to know (*b* about); *hap̄*. to inform.
ydʿ to abandon (? Aḥīqar 44) (Ar. *wdʿ*?).
yhb to give.
yhh see *ḥyh*.
yhw Yᵉhō (H. deity).
yhwd Yᵉhūḏ, Judah (province) (H.); *yhwdy* Jew.
yhwḥn (H. f. proper name [Yᵉhōḥan?]); *yhwḥnn* Yᵉhōḥanan (H.).
ywz revolt (P., Avestan *yaoza*).
ywm day.
yzn, yznyh (H. proper name [Yᵉzanyāh]).
(*yzp*) *zpt* loan.
yṭb *hap̄*. to satisfy.
ykl see *khl*.
yll *hap̄*. *hyll* to lament.
ymʾ to swear; *mwmʾh* oath.
ynq to suck.
yslḥ (H. f. proper name [Yislaḥ]).
ysr *hiṯp*. to be disciplined (impf. *ytsr*).
(*yʿʾ*) *mwʿʾ* (*šmš*) sunrise, east.
(*yʿd*) *ʿdh* assembly.
(*yʿṭ*) *yʿṭ* counselor; *ʿṭh* advice, counsel.
yqd to burn.
yrwšlm Yᵉrūšalem, Jerusalem (H. place name).
yrḥ month.
yšr *hap̄*. (*ʾap̄*.) to send.
ytb to sit.
(*ytr*) *ytyr* more (adverb).

K

k like as. See also *znh, kzy, pm*.
kʾ (proper name of uncertain [Anatolian?] origin).
(*kʾh*) *kʾyh* rebuke.
(*kbb*) *kb* thorn.
kbh to extinguish, to treat lightly.
kbl fetter.
kdb false, forged.
khl, ykl to be able.
khn (Jewish) priest.
kwt, kwtʾ thus.
kzy when, like as, that, so that.
ky for (particle).
kl all, every, entire, *klʾ* altogether.
klb dog.
kmr (pagan) priest.
kn thus.
knbwzy Kanbūziya, Cambyses (P.).
knh (*knt*?) colleague, pl. *knwn* (Akk *kinattu*).
knzsrm treasurer(?) (P.?).
knkr talent (monetary unit).
knt spelt, pl. *kntn*.
ksh *pa*. to cover.
kslw Kislew (Jewish month).
ksp silver, money.
kʿn, kʿnt, kʿt now.
kp hand.
kṣp wrath.
krsʾ throne.
(*krṣ*) *ʾmr krṣy-* to slander (cf. Biblical Aram. *ʾkl qrṣy-*).
krš ten-shekel unit (P. *karša*).
ktb to write.
ktwn cloak, garment.

L

l to, for (direction, dative, accusative, possession, preceding inf.). See also *ʾmr, qbl*.
lʾ not, *blʾ bywmyk* before your time, *hn lʾ* otherwise.
lbb heart.
lbwnh incense (H.).
lbn brick.
lbš to wear (clothes); *lbš* garment.
lhn except.
(*lw*) *hn lw* otherwise.
lḥh evil.
lḥn servant; *lḥnt* maid servant.
lm particle introducing direct speech (< *lmh* why?[?]).
lmh why?; *lmh* (*lmh hn*) lest.
lqbl see *qbl*.
lqḥ to take,—*npš* to kill; *hiṯp*. to be accepted.

M

mbṭḥyh, mbṭḥ (H. f. proper name [Mibṭaḥyāh]).
mgr *pa*. to destroy.

mdbḥ see *dbḥ*.
mh what?, *mh zy* whatever. See also *lmh*.
mwmʾh see *ymʾ*.
mwnq see *ynq*.
mwsrm (proper name prob. of Anatolian origin [Muwasarma]).
mwʿʾ see *yʿʾ*.
mzrq see *zrq*.
mwt (*myt*) to die; *mwt* death.
mḥʾ to beat; *mḥʾh* blow.
mḥzy see *ḥzh*.
mḥsyh, mḥsh Maḥsēyāh (H.).
mḥr tomorrow.
mḥtʾ see *mnḥh*.
mṭʾ to come, to be added (interest).
mṭll see *ṭll*.
myn water, *myʾ qšyʾ* "difficult waters," cataract (loan trans. of Eg. *mw byn*, cf. F. Rundgren, in *Studia Linguistica*, XI [1957], 57—60).
myt see *mwt*.
mlʾ *hitp*. to be filled, to receive full payment.
mlḥ boatman.
mlk king; *mlkw* reign.
(*mll*) *mlh* word, matter, pl. *mln*; *mmll* speech.
mmr see *ʾmr*.
mn from (local), since (temporal), by (agent of passive), than, more than.
mn zy whoever.
mndʿ in *kmndʿ* "like anything" = extraordinarily.
mndʿm anything, (pl. f.) *mndʿmtʾ* things.
mnh *pa*. to employ, to appoint.
mnḥh sacrificial offering, pl. *mnḥtʾ*, *mḥtʾ*.
mnʿl see *ʿll*.
mswrʾ Mesōrē (Eg. month).
mʿrb see *ʿrb*.
mṣph (place name? [reading and meaning uncertain]).
mṣry Egyptian; *mṣryn* Egypt.
mrʾ lord.
mrby see *rbh*.
mrd to revolt.
mrḥšwn Marḥešwan (Jewish month).
(*mrr*) *mryr*, (f.) *mrrtʾ* bitter, *mrr* (Aḥīqar 105) bitter leaves (reading uncertain).
mšʾn (meaning uncertain [shoe, anklet?]).
mšḥ to use oil; *mšḥ* oil.
mšḥh measurement.
mšk hide.
mšlk (H. proper name [Mušlak "foundling"?]).
mšlm Mᵉšullam; *mšlmt* (f.) Mᵉšullamt, Mᵉšullemeṯ (H.).

N

nbwzrʾbn Nabū-zēr-ibni (Akk.).
nbwsmskn Nabū-sum-iskun (Akk.).
ngʿ to touch.
ndn Nādin (Akk.).
ndš *pa*. (?) to tear down.
nḥš copper, bronze.
nḥtḥwr Naḥtiḥūr (Eg.).
nks (pl. *nksn*) property, possessions.
nmʿty *leg*. *nʿmty* "my dear (f.)" (?).
nmr leopard.
(*nsk*) *nsyk* leader (Akk. *nasīku*).
nʿm see *nmʿty*.
npyn (P. [?] proper name).
npq to go out; *hap̄*. to bring out, to take out, to produce, to remove.
npš soul, self, life.
nṣl *hap̄*. (*ʾap̄*.) to take away, to remove.
nʿr to bray.
nšn see *ʿnth*.
nšq *hap̄*. to kindle (wrath) (?).
ntn to give; *ntn* Naṯan (H.).

S

sbl *pa*. to maintain.
sgn prefect (Akk. *šaknu*).
swn Swēn, Assuan (Eg. place name).
swsh horse.
synkšd Sīn-kāšid (Akk.).
skyn knife.
snʾblṭ Sīn-uballiṭ, Sanballat (Akk.).
snh bramble.
snḥʾryb Sīn-aḫḫē-erība, Sanherib (Akk.).
(*spr*) *spr* document; *spr* scribe, secretary.
srw (proper name of uncertain reading [*srn*?], prob. of Anatolian origin).
s^r/_dmnz, *s^r/_dsbnz* (proper names prob. of Anatolian origin).
srys eunuch (Akk. *ša rēši*).

ʿ

ʿbd to make, to do, to serve,—*dyn* to litigate (Akk. *dīnam epēšu*),—*lnpš*- to take for oneself,—*ʿl* to add to, *ʿbyd l* attached to(?); *hitp*. to be done; *ʿbd* servant, slave; *ʿbydh* work, service.
ʿbq, *lʿbq wlʿbq* quickly.
ʿd until, unto (prep., local), *ʿd*, *wʿd* until (prep., temporal), *ʿd*, *ʿd zy*, *zy ʿd* until (conj.).
ʿdh *hap̄*. to remove.
ʿdh see *yʿd*.
ʿdn time.
(*ʿzz*) *ʿzyz* powerful.
ʿzqh seal, signet.
ʿzryh ʿAzaryāh (H.).
ʿṭh see *yʿṭ*.
ʿl to, against, upon, about, concerning, for, *ʿl dbr* concerning, *ʿl zy* because (conj.).
ʿlwh sacrifice.
(*ʿly*) *ʿlyh* upper end (it has been much debated whether this should be interpreted to mean north or south), *ʿlytʾ* Upper Egypt.
ʿll to enter; *hap̄*. to bring in (a dowry).
ʿlm eternity.
(*ʿlm*) *ʿlym* slave.
ʿm (together) with, in connection with.
(*ʿmd*) *ʿmwd* column.
ʿmr wool.
ʿnh to answer.
ʿnwh poverty.
ʿnz she-goat.
ʿnnyh, *ʿnny* ʿAnanyāh (H.).
ʿq timber, wood, pl. *ʿqn*, *ʿqhn*.
(*ʿrb*) *mʿrb* (*šmš*) sunset, west.
(*ʿrb*) *ʿrbn* security.
ʿrh, f. *ʿryh* naked.
ʿrq to meet.
ʿśr ten; *ʿśrtʾ* ten(-shekel piece); *ʿśrn* twenty.
ʿšt *ʾitpa*. to be concerned (*ʿl*, *l* with).
(*ʿštʾ*) *bʿštʾ* (measured) by the one (-cubit measure) (Akk. *ištēn*).
(*ʿtq*) *ʿtyq* old.
ʿtršwry ʿAttaršūrī.

P

pgʿ to meet.
pgr body, corpse.
pḥh governor (Akk. *pīḫatu*, *pāḫatu*).
pṭwsry, *pṭsry* (wrongly *pṭswry*) Petōsirī (Eg.).
pṭḥnwm Peṭḫnūm (Eg.).
pyq (an object belonging to a trousseau, of uncertain meaning).
pyrmʾ see *prymʾ*.
pytrʿnz (proper name prob. of Anatolian origin [Piya-Tarḫunazi]).
plg half.
plḥ to serve.
plṭy Palṭī (H.).
pm mouth, edge (of a knife), *kpm* at the dictation of.
pmwn Pamōn (Eg.).
(*psl*) *pslh*, *psylh* hewn stones.
ppṭʿwnyt (Eg. proper name).
pqd to command; *pqyd* official.
przl iron.
prymʾ, *pyrmʾ* (proper name; if of Anatolian origin, the once attested *pyrmʾ* may be the correct form).
prmwty Pharmūthi (Eg. month).
prʿ to pay; *prʿn* payment.
(*prʿ*) *bpryʿ* in a hurry.
prš (meaning unknown, perhaps the beginning of a Persian word.)
prtrk commander (P. *frataraka*).
pšk span.
pty width.
ptkr statue; *ptkrkr* sculptor (P. *patkara*, *patkarkara*).
ptp rations, provisions (P. *pitpa*).

Ṣ

(*ṣbt*) *ṣbyt* holder (conjectural reading, Akk. *ṣābitu*).
ṣdq to win (a law suit); *ṣdyq* righteous (conjectural reading); *ṣdqh* worldly reward (by the deity); *ṣdq* Ṣadōq (H.).
ṣwm to fast.
ṣyr hinge of a door.
ṣlh *pa*. to pray.
ṣpn *hap̄*. to hide.

Q

qbl to complain (accus., *l*, *qdm* before); *lqbl* in accordance with, *lqbl zy* as (conj.).

qdm, qdmt before (local and temporal); *qdmn, qdmyn, lqdmn, lqdmyn, mn qdmn* formerly.

qwm to rise, to stay; *pa.* to leave standing, intact; *hap̄.* to place.

qwnyh (H. proper name [Qōnīyāh]).

qṭ cash(?) (cf. B. A. Levine, in *Journal of the American Oriental Society*, LXXXIV [1964], 20).

qṭl to kill; *hiṯp.* to be killed; *qṭl* killing.

qnh to acquire.

qrb to draw near; *pa.* to bring near, to present, to offer (sacrifices); *qryb* near, relative; *qrbt* then.

qšh hard, difficult. See also *myn.*

R

r abbreviation of *rbᶜ* quarter.

rᵓš head, beginning, (*rš,* Akk. *rēšu*) capital.

rb master, great man, *rb ḥyl* high officer; great, high (priest), pl. *rbrbn.*

rbh (det.) *rbyᵓ* officer (Akk. *rabū?*).

rbh, rbᵓ to grow up, to become due (interest), to pay interest; *pa.* to bring up; *mrby* interest.

rgl foot.

rḥm to love, to like; (pl.) *rḥmn* mercy, favor; *rḥmn* merciful, kind.

(*rḥq*) *rḥyq* remote, stranger, quit; *mrḥq* quit claim.

rkb rider.

(*rkk*) *rkyk* soft.

rmn pomegranate.

(*rpᵓ*) *rpᵓh* cure.

rš see *rᵓš.*

ršh to start a legal action against.

ršt (P. proper name [Rāšt?]).

Ś

śb old.

(*śgᵓ*) *śgyᵓ* much (adjective and adverb), many.

śhd witness.

śyb see *śb.*

śym to place, to put; *hiṯp.* to be placed (fetter), to be given (order).

śnᵓ to divorce; *śnᵓh* divorce.

śnn (*šnn?*) (meaning uncertain [(pl.) basket, pot < Akk. *sannu,* Ar. *šann* (worn) water bag?]).

śᵓr barley, pl. *śᶜrn.*

śq sackcloth, pl. *śqqn.*

śrp to burn.

śrq cutting.

Š

šᵓl to ask. See also *šlm.*

šᵓr see *šyryt.*

šbh Sabbath(?).

šbq to leave, to let; *hiṯp.* to be left, released.

šdr *pa.* to send (word).

šwh to be equal to, to be worth.

šwšn Śūšan, Shushan (P. place name).

šzb to save.

šyryt remainder(?).

škḥ *hap̄.* (*ᵓap̄.*) to find.

šlḥ to send,—*ᶜl* to send word, write to; *hiṯp.* pass.

(*šlṭ*) *šlyṭ* having full control (*b* over), empowered.

šlm *pa.* to pay back; *šlm* well-being, greetings, *šᵓl šlm* to greet; *šlmyh* Šelemyāh (H.).

šm name, *bšm* in the name of, in behalf of.

šmyn heaven, det. *šmyᵓ.*

šmᶜ to hear, to listen to; *hiṯp.* to be heard, learned about; *šmᶜyh* Šᵉmaᶜyāh (H.).

šmr *hiṯp.* to take heed.

šmryn Šāmrayn, Samaria (H. place name).

šmš sun.

šnh year.

šnn see *śnn.*

šnṣyw see *ṣṣy.*

špṭ to plead.

ṣṣy to succeed (perf. *šnṣyw*).

šql see *tql.*

(*šrr*) *šryr* strong, healthy; *šrrt* strength, prosperity.

šty to drink.

T

tbᵓ (f.) Tabā (Eg.).

tbr to break.

twbᵓ again.

tḥwm border.

tḥwt Thōth (Eg. month).

tḥpy (f.) Taḥapī (Eg.).

tḥt, (*mn*) *tḥt* underneath, instead of; *tḥty*ʾ lower end (cf. *ʿly*), *tḥtyt*ʾ Lower Egypt.
tkl *hit̲p*. (*hit̲pa.*?) to rely.
tly weapons.
tmh there.
tmwz Tammūz (Jewish month).
tmnḥ (f.) devotee (Eg.).
tmt (f.) Tamut (Eg.).
tnh here.
tnyn second.
tʿnpy (proper name prob. of Anatolian origin, ending in *-piya*).
tqbr (reading and meaning uncertain).
tql (*šql*) shekel.
tqm castor oil (Eg.).
tryn two. See also *tnyn*.
trk *pa.* to drive out.
trʿ door.

III. BIBLICAL ARAMAIC

(H. L. Ginsberg)

(* indicates that the particular form of a word so marked does not occur in Biblical Aramaic texts.

The gender of nouns which do not designate living beings is indicated where-ever it can be determined from the context.)

א

*אַב father, ancestor, suff. אֲבִי, אֲבוּךְ, אֲבוּהִי, pl. אֲבָהָתִי, ־תָךְ, ־תַנָא.

*אֵב (m.) fruit, suff. אִנְבֵּהּ.

*אֲבַד to perish (impf. *יֵאבְדוּן D 2:18 [conjecture], juss. יֵאבַדוּ); *hap̄.* to destroy (impf. יְהֹבְדוּן, inf. לְהוֹבָדָה); *hop̄.* to be destroyed (perf. הוּבַד).

אֶבֶן (f.) stone, det. אַבְנָא.

אִגְּרָה (f.) letter, communication, det. אִגַּרְתָּא (Akk.).

אֱדַיִן then, next, בֵּאדַיִן thereupon, forthwith.

אֲדָר Adar (month).

*אִדַּר threshing floor, pl. אִדְּרֵי.

*אֲדַרְגָּזַר counselor, pl. אֲדָרְגָּזְרַיָּא (P.).

אַדְרַזְדָּא diligently (P.).

אֶדְרָע in בְּאֶדְרָע וְחָיִל by force and might, forcibly. See דְּרָע.

אַזְדָּא (predicative adj., originally an adverb) made known, declared, decreed (P.).

*אֲזָה to fire, to stoke (a furnace) (inf. לְמֵזֵא, לְמֵזְיֵהּ, part. pass. אֲזֵה).

אֲזַל to go (imp. אֱזֶל E 5:14) (impf. and inf. are supplied by הלך).

*אַח brother, kinsman, fellow priest (because the Jewish priests constitute a caste, or kindred), pl. suff. אֶחָיךְ.

*אֲחִידָה riddle.

*אַחֲוָיָה explaining (action noun). See חוי.

אַחְמְתָא Ecbatana (city, P. Hagmatāna).

אַחֲרֵי after (prep.), suff. אַחֲרֵיהֹן.

אָחֳרִי see אָחֳרָן.

*אַחֲרִי end (only in בְּאַחֲרִית יוֹמַיָּא ["at the end of time"] in time to come [Hebraism ?]).

אָחֳרֵין in וְעַד – finally.

אָחֳרָן, f. אָחֳרִי another.

*אֲחַשְׁדַּרְפַּן satrap, pl. אֲחַשְׁדַּרְפְּנַיָּא (P.).

אִילָן (m.) tree, det. אִילָנָא.

*אֵימְתָן, f. אֵימְתָנִי frightful, terrifying.

אִיתַי there is, there are, –ל – to have, –דִּי it is the case that (E 5:17); (with suff. and a following participle) to be (with emphasis) (e.g. הַאִיתָ֫יךְ כָּהֵל "*are* you able?")

אֲכַל to eat, to devour (perf. אֲכַ֫לוּ, impf. תֵּאכֻל, part. אָכְלָה, imp. אֲכֻ֫לִי).

אַל not (with wishes and commands).

אֵל (Q E 5:15), אֵלֶּה, אִלֵּ(י)ן these.

אֱלָה god (with ו: בֵּאלָהֵהּ ,ב ,כ ,ל, and etc., but אֱלָהּ שְׁמַיָּא (לֶאֱלָהּ שְׁמַיָּא), the God of Heaven (official designation of the God of the Jews), בַּר אֱלָהִין a divine being. (The pl. never has sg. meaning as in H.)

אֲלוּ, אֲרוּ (interjection lo!) there was/were (in the recording of dreams and visions).

אִלֵּ(י)ן see אֵל, אֵ֫לֶּה.

אִלֵּךְ those.

אֲלַף thousand, cstr. אֲ֫לֶף, det. אַלְפָּא "the thousand" (not accompanied by a noun), pl. K (Hebraizing) אלפים Q אַלְפִין.

אַמָּה (f.) cubit, pl. אַמִּין.

אֻמָּה (f.) nation, pl. אֻמַּיָּא (אֻמַּיָּא, cf. חַרְטֹם).

אמן *hap̄.* to trust in (הֵימִן בְּ־), part. pass. מְהֵימַן trustworthy (D 2:45), loyal, faithful (D 6:5).

אֲמַר to say, to tell, to command (perf. אֲמֶ֫רֶת, אַמְרֵת, impf. יֵאמַר, imp. אֱמַר, inf. לְמֵ(א)מַר, (E 5:8) "as follows").

אִמַּר lamb, pl. אִמְּרִין.

אִנְבֵּהּ see *אֵב*.

אֲנָה I.

אִנּוּן, f. אִנִּין they, them, those. Cf. הוּא.

אֱנוֹשׁ K אֱנוֹשָׁא mankind (D 4:13, 14).

אֲנַ֫חְנָא, אֲנַ֫חְנָה we.

אִנִּין see אִנּוּן.

אֲנַס to baffle.

אַנְפִּין (pl. only) face, suff. אַנְפּ֫וֹהִי.

אֱנָשׁ person, human being, det. אֲנָשָׁא mankind (see *אֱנוֹשׁ*), pl. אֲנָשִׁים (Hebraism) men, human beings. בַּר־אֱנָשׁ man, human being, pl. det. בְּנֵי אֲנָשָׁא.

אַנְתְּ, אַנְתָּה, pl. אַנְתּוּן you (m.).

אַנְתָּה woman, wife, pl. *נְשִׁין*, נְשֵׁיהוֹן.

אֱסוּר fetter, chain, pl. אֱסוּרִין imprisonment.

אָסְנַפַּר (prob. to be emended to אסרבנפר) Ashurbanipal.

אָסְפַּ֫רְנָא exactly, strictly, perfectly (P.).

אֱסָר interdict, prohibition.

אָע (m.) wood, timber, beam.

אַף, וְאַף also, moreover.

אֲפָרְסָי Persian (?), pl. אֲפָרְסָיֵא (E 4:9). Prob. rd. סִפְרָיֵא Sipparites (the initial א due to dittography).

*אֲפָרְסָכָי Persian, pl. אֲפָרְסְכָיֵא (P.).

*אֲפַרְסַתְכָי official, officer, pl. אֲפַרְסַתְכָיֵא (E 4:9). The phrase [?]דִּינָיֵא[!] וְאַפְרְסָתְכַיָּא is perhaps modeled on שֹׁפְטִים וְשֹׁטְרִים, Deut. 16:18).

אַפְּתֹם surely or ultimately (Akk. or P.).

*אֶצְבַּע (f.) finger, toe, pl. אֶצְבְּעָן, אֶצְבְּעָתָא, אֶצְבְּעָת.

אַרְבְּעָה, f. אַרְבַּע four.

*אַרְגְּוָן purple (wool), det. אַרְגְּוָנָא "the purple" (worn by the highest dignitaries).

אֲרוּ see אֲלוּ.

*אֲרַח way, pl. *אֹרְחָן, אֹרְחָתֵהּ.

אַרְיֵה (m.) lion, pl. *אַרְיָוָן, אַרְיָוָתָא.

אַרְיוֹךְ Arioch (prob. P.).

אֲרִיךְ proper (< P. *aryaka* ?).

*אֳרֶךְ length, suff. (conjecture) *אָרְכֵּהּ, E 6:3.

*אַרְכֻבָּה (f.) knee.

אַרְכָה (f.) extension, prolongation (of life).

*אַרְכְּוָי Erechite, pl. ארכוי (Q אַרְכְּוָיֵא, E 4:9), but perhaps to be emended to אַרְכָּיֵי (sg. *אַרְכָּי.)

*אֲרַע (f.) earth, det. אַרְעָא.

ארעא (Q אֲרַע) below (followed by מִן. On the analogy of עִלָּא, the K is probably אַרְעָא).

*אַרְעִי bottom, cstr. אַרְעִית.

אַרְקָא the earth (historical spelling of אַרְעָא).

אַרְתַּחְשַׁשְׂתְּא, אַרְתַּחְשַׁסְתְּא Artaxerxes (P. Artaḫšaśa).

*אֹשׁ (m.) foundation, pl. אֻשַּׁיָּא, אֻשּׁוֹהִי.

אֶשָּׁא fire.

אָשַׁף enchanter, pl. אָשְׁפִין (Akk.).

אָשַּׁרְנָא (det.)(m.) furnishings (prob. P.).

אֶשְׁתַּדּוּר (m.) insurrection (Akk. or P.).

אִשְׁתִּי (root שתי, with prothetic א) to drink (perf. אִשְׁתִּיו, part. שָׁתַיִן).

*אָת (m.) sign, portent.

אֲתָה, אֲתָא to come (imp. אֱתוֹ, inf. לְמֵתֵא); *hap̄.* to bring (perf. הַיְתִי, הַיְתִיו, inf. לְהַיְתָיָה); *hop̄.* to be brought (perf. הֵיתָיִת, הֵיתַיו).

אַתּוּן (m.) furnace (Akk.).

אֲתַר (m.) place (D 2:35: trace ?), suff. אַתְרֵהּ; אֲתַר דִּי where (relative). See also בָּאתַר.

ב

בְּ (בַּ, בֶּ, etc.) in, with (by means of), in the matter of.

בֵּאדַיִן thereupon, forthwith. See also אֱדַיִן.

*בְּאִישׁ bad, evil, f. det. בִּאישְׁתָּא.

בְּאֵשׁ to be bad, עֲלוֹהִי - he was grieved, displeased.

בָּאתַר, בָּתַר (< *בַּאֲתַר) after (prep.), suff. בָּתְרָךְ.

בָּבֶל (f.) Babylon; in E 5:17, 6:1, 7:16, D 2:48 f., 3:1, 12, 30: Babylonia (in E 5:17, 6:1 Susiana and Media are included, witness 6:2; so perhaps in all cases).

*בָּבְלָי Babylonian, pl. בָּבְלָיֵא.

בדר *pa.* to scatter (imp. בַּדַּרוּ).

בְּהִילוּ haste.

בהל *hitp.* inf. (noun of action) הִתְבְּהָלָה haste; *pa.* to upset, to perturb, to disquiet (impf. suff. יְבַהֲלֻנַּנִי, יְבַהֲלֻנֵּהּ, juss. suff. יְבַהֲלָךְ); *hitpa.* to be upset, perturbed, agitated (part. מִתְבָּהַל).

בּוֹזְנַי see שְׁתַר - .

*בְּטֵל (*בְּטִל) to cease, to be idle (perf. בְּטֵלַת, part. בָּטְלָא); *pa.* to make (somebody) desist, to make (somebody) stop (doing something) (perf. בַּטִּלוּ, inf. לְבַטָּלָא, דִּי לָא לְבַטָּלָא "without fail").

*בַּי (*בֵּי) (m.) house, palace, temple, cstr. בֵּית, det. בַּיְתָא, suff. בַּיְתֵהּ, pl. suff. בָּתֵּיכוֹן; בֵּית מַלְכָּא, E 6:4 the royal treasury; בֵּית מַלְכוּ, D 4:27 a royal residence; *בֵּית מִשְׁתֵּא (det. בֵּית מִשְׁתְּיָא) banquet hall; *בֵּית אֱלָהּ (det. בֵּית אֱלָהָא) temple; *בֵּית גנז repository (pl. det. בֵּית גִּנְזַיָּא, with only the second element taking the pl. ending, cf. H. בֵּית אָבוֹת); on the supposed בֵּית סִפְרַיָּא, see n. to E 6:1.

בֵּין among, suff. Q בֵּינֵיהֵין.

בִּינָה understanding, discernment.

בִּירָה fortress, det. בִּירְתָא (Akk.).

בית to spend the night (perf. בָּת).

בָּל mind.

בֵּלשַׁאצַּר see בֵּלְאשַׁצַּר.

*בליּ *pa.* to wear out, to molest (impf. יְבַלֵּא) (read יְסַלֵּא "he will despise" ?).

בְּלוֹ a kind of tax, tribute? (Akk.).

בֵּלְטְשַׁאצַּר Belteshazzar (Akk.).

בֵּלְשַׁאצַּר (D 7:1: בלאשצר) Belshazzar (Akk.).

*בְּנָה to build, to rebuild, to fortify (a city) (perf. suff. בְּנָהִי, בֱּנַיְתַהּ, inf. לִבְנֵא, לְמִבְנֵא, לְמִבְנְיָה (read לְמִבְנְיֵהּ ?), part. בָּנַיִן, pass. בְּנֵה).

בְּנִי, בְּנוֹהִי, etc., see בַּר.

*בִּנְיָן (m.) edifice.

בְּנַס to be vexed, to lose patience.

בְּעָא, בְּעָה to look for, to ask for, to request, to seek, to want, to try, to be on the point of (D 2:13) (perf. בְּעוֹ, בְּעֵינָא, part. בָּעֵא, בָּעֵה, בָּעַיִן, impf. יִבְעֵא, אֶבְעֵא, inf. לְמִבְעֵא), בָּעוּ – to address (offer) a petition (מִן to); *pa.* to seek out, to turn to (impf. יְבַעוֹן).

בָּעוּ petition, prayer, suff. בָּעוּתֵהּ.

בְּעֵל טְעֵם official in charge (adapted from Akk. *bēl ṭēmi* and felt to be too foreign to be put in the det. state).

*בִּקְעָה plain.

*בַּקַּר *pa.* to search, to investigate (perf. בַּקַּרוּ, impf. יְבַקַּר); *hiṯpa.* יִתְבַּקַּר let a search be made.

בַּר son, child, suff. בְּרֵהּ, pl. *בְּנִין, בְּנֵי, etc.; ... בַּר שְׁנִין ... years old, מִן בְּנֵי גָלוּתָא a member of the exile community. See also אֱלָהּ, אֱנָשׁ, תּוֹר.

*בַּר (root *brr*) the (open) field, the open, the outdoors, det. בָּרָא.

*בְּרֵךְ knee, pl. suff. בִּרְכוֹהִי.

ברך (prob. $^{i}/_{e}$ class) to kneel (part. בָּרֵךְ ["he would get down on his knees"]).

בָּרֵךְ *pa.* (of the preceding ?) to bless, to praise (with God as object) (part. pass. מְבָרַךְ).

בְּרַם but, however.

בְּשַׂר (m.) flesh, mortals, creatures, det. בִּשְׂרָא.

*בַּת bath (name of a liquid measure), pl. בַּתִּין.

בָּתַר see באתר.

ג

*גַּב (*גְּנַב) only in D 7:6 עַל גַּבַּיהּ "on its sides" or "on its back."

גֹּב animal pit, det. גֻּבָּא.

*גְּבוּרָה (f). power, might, det. גְּבוּרְתָא.

גְּבַר man, pl. גֻּבְרִין, גֻּבְרַיָּא.

*גִּבָּר mighty, pl. גִּבָּרֵי־חַיִל D 3:20 (H. גִּבֹּרֵי כֹחַ, Ps. 103:20) powerful (lit., mighty of strength).

גְּדָבַר treasurer, pl. גְּדָבְרַיָּא (P.).

גדד to cut down (imp. גֹּדּוּ).

גּוֹא inside, interior, always preceded by prep.: לְגוֹא into, מִן גּוֹא out of, בְּגַוַּהּ therein.

גֵּוָה (root גאי) arrogance.

גוח *ap̄.* to stir up (part. מְגִיחָן).

גְּזַבַר treasurer, pl. גִּזַּבְרַיָּא (P.).

גזר (*h*)*iṯp.* D 2:34, 45 הִ(א)תְגְּזֶרֶת, usually translated (following H. גזר "to cut [to pieces]") "was cut out, broke off," but this assumes omission of "and was hurled" or "and rolled"; therefore, perhaps to be connected with Aram.

גַּנְדֵּר "to roll (trans.)."

*גָּזַר soothsayer, exorcizer (or the like), pl. גָּזְרִין, גָּזְרַיָּא.

*גְּזֵרָה decree (H.).

*גִּיר plaster, whitewash.

*גַּלְגַּל wheel (of the Deity's throne-chariot, cf. Ezek. 1:15-21; 10:1 ff.), pl. גַּלְגִּלּוֹהִי.

*גְּלָה to reveal (part. גָּלֵא, inf. לְמִגְלֵא); *p*ᵓᶜ*īl* to be revealed (גְּלִי, in pause גֱּלִי); *hap̄.* to deport, to exile (perf. הַגְלִי).

*גָּלוּ exile community, det. גָּלוּתָא.

גְּלָל in אֶבֶן גְּלָל dressed stone.

גְּמִיר et cetera (i.e., "and the rest of the customary salutation").

*גנב see גַּב.

*גְּנַז deposit, treasure, see *בַּיִ (P.).

*גַּף (f.) wing, pl. גַּפִּין, גַּפִּיה.

*גְּרַם (*גְּרֵם ?) bone, pl. גַּרְמֵיהוֹן.

*גְּשֵׁם (m.) body, suff. גֶּשְׁמְהוֹן, גִּשְׁמֵהּ.

ד

דְּ see דִּי.

דָּא (f.), m. דְּנָה, pl. אִלֵּין, this, דָּא לְדָא against each other, דְּנָה עִם דְּנָה together.

דֹּב bear.

*דְּבַח to sacrifice (part. דָּבְחִין).

*דְּבַח sacrifice, pl. דִּבְחִין.

*דְּבִק to cling, to hold fast (part. דָּבְקִין), דְּנָה עִם דְּנָה — to hold together.

דִּבְרַת in עַל (<עַד) דִּבְרַת דִּי to the end that.

דְּהַב gold, det. דַּהֲבָא(ה).

דהוא (E 4:9, Q דֶּהָיֵא, as if pl. m. of a gentilic) = דְּהוּא or דִּי הוּא "that is."

דור to dwell (part. דארין, Q דָּיְרִין, impf. ידרון, Q יְדוּרָן).

דּוּרָא Dura (name of a plain).

דוש to trample (impf. suff. תְּדוּשִׁנַּהּ).

דַּחֲוָן (D 6:19) dining-board, portable table (cf. H. pl. דחוונות *Tosephta Kelim, Baba Meṣiᶜa* 5:3; Rashi and David Qimḥi, *Book of Roots,* end, *s.v.*; *דַּחֲוָה [pl. דַּחֲוָן] "concubine" is unattested).

*דְּחִל to fear (part. דָּחֲלִין, pass. דְּחִיל, דְּחִילָה terrible, frightful); *pa.* to frighten (impf. suff. יְדַחֲלִנַּנִי).

דִּי (דְּ) of (an "of" phrase is equivalent to an adjective, and the noun governed by "of" assumes the det. state wherever an adjective would; e. g. "its legs were of iron" is רַגְלוֹהִי ... דִּי פַרְזֶל, D 2:33, but "its iron legs" is רַגְלוֹהִי דִּי פַרְזְלָא, D 2:34). דִּי לְ- forms independent possessive pronouns: דִּי לֵהּ his (D 2:20). — Relative particle (see also דהוא and דִּי לָא "without"); — (conj.) that, because, for, since (pleonastic in this sense in דִּי לְמָה E 7:23 = לְמָה E 4:22 "lest"). Also introduces direct quotations. — דִּי following a prep. or some other governing word forms subordinating conjunctions, see לָקֳבֵל דִּי, הֵא כְדִי, כְּדִי, דִּבְרַת, עַד דִּי, מִן דִּי, כָּל קֳבֵל דִּי.

דִּי לָא without (prep.).

דין to judge (part. דאנין, Q. דָּיְנִין).

דִּין (m.) justice, tribunal, det. דִּינָא(ה).

*דַּיָּן judge, pl. דַּיָּנִין, *דַּיָּנַיָּא E 4:9 (conjecture, for דִּינָיֵא).

דִּינָיֵא (vocalized as a gentilic, but see דַּיָּן).

דֵּךְ, f. דָּךְ, דִּכֵּן (m. and f.), pl. אִלֵּךְ that (demonstrative adjective).

*דְּכַר ram, pl. דִּכְרִין.

*דִּכְרוֹן memorandum.

*דָּכְרָן in סְפַר דָּכְרָנַיָּא "the Annals."

דָּלִק (part.) flaming.

דמי to resemble (part. דָּמְיָה, דָּמֵה).

דְּנָה this, see דָּא.

דָּנִיֵּאל Daniel.

דקק to crumble (perf. דָּקוּ, var. דַּקּוּ); *hap̄.* to pulverize (perf. הַדֶּקֶת and הַדֶּקֶת, impf. תַּדִּק, part. מְהַדֵּק, מַדֱּקָה and מַדֱּקָה).

דָּר generation, age, עִם דָּר וְדָר throughout the ages.

דָּרְיָוֶשׁ Darius (P. Dārayavauš).

*דְּרָע arm, pl. דְּרָעוֹהִי. Cf. אֶדְרָע.

דָּת (f.) law, pl. דָּתֵי (P.).

*דְּתַא(?) grass, herbage, det. דִּתְאָא.

*דְּתָבַר law official, pl. דְּתָבְרַיָּא (P.).

ה

הֲ (as in הֲלָא), הַ (before laryngal or vowelless consonant) particle introducing question calling for a yes-or-no answer. See also הַצְדָא.

הָא (interjection) look! but . . . !

הֵא כְדִי as, in the same way that.

*הַדָּבַר companion, pl. הַדָּבְרוֹהִי (P.).

*הַדָּם limb, pl. הַדָּמִין; עֲבַד הַדָּמִין to hack to pieces, to quarter (P.).

*הַדַּר *pa.* to extol, to glorify (perf. הַדַּרְתָּ, part. מְהַדַּר).

*הֲדַר glory, det. הַדְרָא, suff. הַדְרִי (הַדְרִי D 4:33, perhaps read *הַדְרֵת "I returned [intrans.]").

הוּא, f. הִיא he, she, that (demonstrative pronoun and adjective).

הֲוָא, הֲוָה to be, to remain, to happen, also an auxiliary verb combining with part. to express continued, habitual, or repeated action (perf. הֲוׄ, impf. לֶהֱוֵה, לֶהֱוֺן, לֶהֶוְיָן, imp. הֱוׄ); הֲוָה לְ- to become, to turn into.

*הוך (apparent root of מְהָךְ and יְהָךְ, see הלך).

הִיא see הוּא.

*הֵיכַל palace, temple, det. הֵיכְלָא (Akk.).

הֵימִן see אמן.

הַיְתִי see אֲתָא.

הלך to go (to or from somewhere, contrast *pa.*) (confined to inf. מְהָךְ [for *מֶהֱלַךְ] and impf. יְהָךְ; perf., part., and imp. supplied by אזל); *pa.* to walk (without reference to starting point or goal) (part. מְהַלֵּךְ, מַהְלְכִין (< מְהַלְּכִין < מְהַלְּכִין).

הֲלָךְ a certain impost (Akk.).

הִמּוֹ they, them.

הִמּוֹן them.

*הַמְיָנֵךְ necklace, det. *הַמְיָנְכָא (K המונכא, Q הַמְנִיכָא).

הֵן if; הֵן ... הֵן ... וְהֵן whether ...or... or.

הַצְדָּא really ? (often explained as the interrogative particle הֲ plus *צְדָא, from *yṣd, Ar. *waṣada* "to be firm").

*הַרְהֹר, pl. הַרְהֹרִין imaginings.

*הִתְנַדָּבָה voluntary contribution, cstr. הִתְנַדָּבוּת (*hiṯpa.* inf. of נדב, used as a noun of action and hence a designation of the product of action).

ו

וְ (also וַ, וֶ, וֵ, וָ, or וּ) most commonly equivalent to English "and" but often to be rendered by, e.g., "but" (e.g., E 5:5, the first וְ), "then" (E 5:1, the first וְ), "so" (E 6:14), "as" (D 4:16, 19 "as his thoughts upset him"), or "further" (E 7:24 "you are further advised"). Note the hendiadys פֻּקוּ וֶאֱתוֹ "come out here" (D 3:26, lit. "come out and come"), נָגֵד וְנָפֵק "gushed forth" (D 7:10, lit. "was flowing and coming out").

ז

*זְבַן to buy (part. זָבְנִין).

*זְהִיר wary, וּזְהִירִין הֱוׄ "and beware of (practicing any guile in this matter)."

זיד/זוד *hap̄.* to act impiously (inf. לַהֲזָדָה).

זון *hiṯp.* to get one's food (from), to live on (impf. יִתְּזִין [מִן]).

זוע to tremble (part. זאעין, Q זָיְעִין).

*זִיו (m.) splendor, radiance, pl. face.

זָכוּ (f.) innocence.

זְכַרְיָה Zechariah.

זמן *hitp.* to band together (perf. הזמנתון, see n. to D 2:9).

זְמָן, זְמַן (m.) time (both "temps" and "fois"), pl. זִמְנִין.

*זְמָר music.

*זַמָּר musician.

*זַן kind, sort, pl. זְנֵי (P.).

*זְעֵיר, f. זְעֵירָה little, small.

זְעִק to cry out.

*זְקַף to erect or to impale (part. pass. זְקִיף).

זְרֻבָּבֶל Zerubbabel.

זְרַע seed.

ח

חֲבוּלָה harm, damage.

חבל *pa.* to harm, to destroy (perf. suff. חַבְּלוּנִי, imp. suff. חַבְּלוּהִי, inf. לְחַבָּלָה); *hitpa.* to be destroyed (impf. תִּתְחַבַּל).

חֲבָל (m.) damage, injury.

*חֲבַר companion, pl. חַבְרוֹהִי.

*חַבְרָה companion (f.), pl. חַבְרָתַהּ ("its fellows," i.e.) "the others" (D 7:20).

חַגַּי Haggai.

חַד, f. חֲדָה one; חַד שִׁבְעָה seven times (as much or more); כַּחֲדָה together.

*חֲדַיִן (pl., or dual., only?) breast, chest, suff. חֲדוֹהִי.

חֶדְוָה joy.

חֲדַת new (E 6:4, but read חַד with LXX).

חוי *pa.* and *hap̄.* to tell, to state, to make known (impf. suff. יְחַוִּנַּהּ, תְּהַחֲוֻנַּנִי, etc.) (the person who is told is expressed either by a pronominal suff. or by לְ plus a noun). See also *אַחֲוָיָה.

חיט/חוט see יחט.

חִוָּר white, pure (of freshly fallen snow).

חֲזָה to see (perf. חֲזַיְתָה, חֲזֵיתוּן, part. חָזֵה, חָזַיִן, pass. חֲזֵה "proper").

*חֱזוּ (m.) vision, appearance, det. חֶזְוָא, suff. חֶזְוִי, חֶזְוֵהּ, pl. חֶזְוֵי.

*חֲזוֹ visibility, suff. חֲזוֹתֵהּ.

חטי *pa.* to offer as an offering of purification (inf. לחטיא, Q לְחַטָּאָה).

*חֲטָי sin, suff. חטיך, Q חֲטָאָךְ.

*חַי living, det. חַיָּא, pl. חַיַּיָּא; חַי עָלְמָא "He who lives forever."

*חֲיָה to live (imp. חֱיִי); *hap̄.* to bring to life, to let live (part. מַחֵא).

חֵיוָה (f.) animal, beast (sg. חֵיוְתָא and חֵיוַת בָּרָא used collectively: "the beasts," "the beasts of the field"), pl. חֵיוָן, etc.

חַיִּין (pl. only) life, cstr. חַיֵּי.

חַיִל (in pause חָיִל) strength, force, army, cstr. חֵיל שְׁמַיָּא "the host of heaven," בְּחַיִל loudly. See also אֶדְרָע.

חַכִּים wise, (noun) wise man, sage.

חָכְמָה wisdom.

חֵלֶם (m.) dream, det. חֶלְמָא.

*חֲלַף to pass by, to elapse (impf. יַחְלְפוּן).

חֲלָק share.

חֱמָה (but וַחֲמָה) wrath.

חֲמַר wine, det. חַמְרָא.

*חִנְטָה wheat (plant or single grain), pl. חִנְטִין wheat (a field or quantity of).

*חֲנֻכָּה inauguration.

חנן to show kindness, mercy to (inf. as noun of action מִחַן); *hitpa.* to implore (part. מִתְחַנַּן).

חֲנַנְיָה Hananiah.

חַסִּיר wanting, deficient.

חסן *hap̄.* to possess, to take possession of (perf. הֶחֱסִנוּ, impf. יַחְסְנוּן).

*חֲסֵן power, might, det. חִסְנָא.

חֲסַף earthenware, pottery, det. חַסְפָּא.

חצף *hap̄.* part. f. (active or passive ?) מְהַחְצְפָה, מַחְצְפָה urgent, pressing.

*חֲרִב to be reduced to (lie in) ruins; *hop̄.* to be destroyed (city or edifice) (perf. הָחָרְבַת).

חַרְטֹם magician, pl. חַרְטֻמִּין, but det. חַרְטֻמַיָּא (cf. אֻמָּה).

*חֲרַךְ *hitpa.* to be singed (perf. הִתְחָרַךְ).

*חֲרַץ hip, loins, suff. חַרְצֵהּ.

*חֲשַׁב to esteem (part. pass. חֲשִׁיבִין).

*חֲשׁוֹךְ darkness.

*חֲשַׁח needing, needed, pl. חַשְׁחִין, f. חַשְׁחָן "things needed."

*חַשְׁחוּ needs, cstr. חַשְׁחוּת.

*חֲשַׁל to smash (part. חָשֵׁל).

*חֲתַם to seal (perf. suff. חַתְמַהּ).

ט

טְאֵב to be good, עֲלוֹהִי – he was pleased (the impf. is supplied by יטב).

טָב good, דְּהַב טָב pure gold, הֵן עַל מַלְכָּא טָב "if it please Your Majesty."

*טַבָּח in רַב טַבָּחַיָּא captain of the (body-)guard.

טוּר (m.) mountain.

טְוָת fasting (adv.).

*טִין clay.

טַל (dew) rain.

טלל (*h*)*ap̄.* to seek shelter (impf. תְּטְלֵל, but this formation, instead of *תְּהַטֵּל or *תַּטֵּל, from a geminate root, is unexampled. Prob. vocalize *hitpa.* תִּטַּלַּל, or *hitp.* תִּטְּלַל).

טעם *pa.* to feed (trans.) (impf. יְטַעֲמוּן, suff. יְטַעֲמוּנֵּהּ).

טְעֵם (m.) (cstr. before "God" טַ֫עַם, otherwise טְעֵם) order, decree, report, influence (of wine); mind, reason, שָׂם טְעֵם to decree, to pay attention, הֲתִיב עֵטָא וּטְעֵם to take counsel (לְ־ with).

*טְפַר fingernail, claw, pl. טִפְרוֹ֫הִי.

*טְרַד to drive away (part. טָרְדִין); *pᵊʿīl* טְרִיד to be driven away.

טַרְפְּלָיֵא (pl. det.) an unidentified class of persons.

י

יבל *hap̄.* to bring, to convey (perf. הֵיבֵל, inf. לְהֵיבָלָה). See also סובל.

*יַבְּשָׁה, det. יַבֶּשְׁתָּא the dry land, the earth.

יְגַר pile, heap (of stones).

יַד (f.) hand, power, det. יְדָא, יְדָה, suff. יְדִי, יְדָךְ, יְדְהֹם, dual יְדַ֫יִן (may include the arm).

ידי (*h*)*ap̄.* to praise, to laud (part. מְהוֹדֵא, מוֹדֵא).

יְדַע to know, to find (out), to realize, to note (perf. יִדְעֵת, impf. אִנְדַּע, תִּנְדַּע, יִנְדְּעוּן, imp. דַּע, part. יָדַע, pass. יְדִ֫יעַ); *hap̄.* to tell, to make (perf. הוֹדַע, part. מְהוֹדְעִין, etc.).

יְהַב to give, to deliver, to lay (foundations, cf. יחט) (imp. הַב, part. יָהֵב, יָהֲבִין, inf. and impf. supplied by נתן); *pᵊʿīl* יְהִיב, יְהִיבַת to be given, consigned; *hitp.* to be given, delivered, provided (impf. יִתְיְהִב, תִּתְיְהִב(הֵ)ב, part. מִתְיְהֵב, etc.).

יְהוּד (the province of) Judah.

*יְהוּדָי Jew, Jewish, pl. יְהוּדָאִין, יְהוּדָיֵא.

יוֹם day, det. יוֹמָא, pl. יוֹמִין, cstr. יוֹמֵי but יוֹמָת עָלְמָא, det. יוֹמַיָּא days, time, יוֹם בְּיוֹם daily.

יוֹצָדָק Jozadak.

יחט (?) *pa.* יַחִ֫יטוּ (for יַחִ֫טוּ?) to lay (foundations?), read יְהִ֫יבוּ?.

יטב serves as impf. (יֵיטַב) of טְאֵב, see above.

יְכִל to be able, to prevail (לְ־ over) (perf. יְכֵ֫לְתָּ, impf. יִכֻל and יוּכַל, part. יָכִל, יָכְלָה).

*יַם (m.) sea, det. יַמָּא.

יסף *hop̄* to be added (perf. הוּסְפַת).

יעט *itpa.* to take counsel and agree (perf. אִתְיָ֫עַטוּ).

*יָעֵט counselor, pl. יָעֲטוֹ֫הִי.

יצב *pa.* to ascertain (inf. לְיַצָּבָא).

יַצִּיב certain, יַצִּיבָא certainty.

יקד to burn, to consume (said of fire) (part. f. det. יָקִדְתָּא, var. יָקֶדְתָּא).

*יְקֵדָה in יְקֵדַת אֶשָּׁא burning (consuming) fire.

*יַקִּיר, f. יַקִּירָה magnificent, difficult, m. det. יַקִּירָא.

יְקָר (var. יְקַר) honor.

יְרוּשְׁלֶם Jerusalem.

יְרַח (m.) month, pl. יַרְחִין.

*יְרֵךְ(?) (*יַרְכָה?) thigh, pl. יַרְכָתֵהּ.

יִשְׂרָאֵל (the people) Israel.

יֵשׁוּעַ Jeshua.

*יָת particle introducing the direct object, suff. יָתְהוֹן.

יְתִב to sit (impf. יִתִּב); *hap̄.* to settle (trans. with personal object) (perf. הוֹתֵב).

יַתִּיר, f. יַתִּירָא exceeding, surpassing, (adv.) יַתִּירָא(ה), יַתִּירָה exceedingly, tremendously.

כ

כְּ (כִּ, כַּ) like, according. Hence it can serve to mark an expression as predicative, or adverbial, as in D 6:1. Closely related to this is its function of reinforcing phrases formed by לָקֳבֵל and the word(s) it governs, e.g. לָקֳבֵל דְּנָה > כָּל־קֳבֵל דְּנָה (< כְּלָקֳבֵל דְּנָה). See further כְּעֶת, כְּעֶנֶת, כְּעַן, כַּחֲדָה, כְּדִי.

*כְּדֵב, f. כִּדְבָה false, lying.

כְּדִי when. See also הֵא כְדִי.

כָּה here. See עַד.

כהל to be able (part. כָּהֵל, כָּהֲלִין).

*כָּהֵן (Jewish) priest, pl. כָּהֲנַיָּא.

*כַּוָּה (f.) window, pl. כַּוִּין.

כּוֹרֶשׁ Cyrus (P. Kūruš).

כַּחֲדָה together, see חַד.

*כַּכַּר talent (unit of weight or money), pl. כַּכְּרִין.

כֹּל, כָּל־ (lit. "the totality of") all, any, det. כֹּלָּא (lit. "the entirety") all, everybody, everything, שְׁלָמָא כֹלָּא all well-being.

כָּל־קֳבֵל (see כְּ) in ־ דְּנָה accordingly, thereupon, and ־ דִּי inasmuch as, because, (D 6:11) just as, (D 5:22) although.

כלל see שכלל.

כְּמָה how!

כֵּן thus.

*כְּנָה (?) (*כְּנָת?) colleague, pl. כְּנָוָתֵהּ, כְּנָוָתְהוֹן.

כְּנֵמָא thus, so, as follows.

*כְּנַשׁ to assemble (trans.) (inf. לְמִכְנַשׁ); *hitpa.* to assemble (intrans.) (part. מִתְכַּנְּשִׁין).

*כַּסְדָּיֵ see כַּשְׂדָּי.

כְּסַף silver, det. כַּסְפָּא.

כְּעַן, כְּעֶנֶת, כְּעֶת now, now then.

כפת *p*ᵊ*'īl* (כְּפִתוּ) to be bound; pa. to bind (part. pass. מְכַפְּתִין).

*כֹּר kor (a dry measure).

*כַּרְבְּלָה hat.

כרי *itp.* to be troubled (perf. אֶתְכְּרִיַּת).

*כָּרוֹז herald.

כרז *hap̄.* to proclaim (perf. הַכְרִזוּ).

*כָּרְסֵא (m.) throne, suff. כָּרְסְיֵהּ, pl. כָּרְסָוָן.

כַּשְׂדָּי (*כַּסְדָּיֵ) Chaldean (D 3:8, 5:30, E 5:12), astrologer (in all other passages).

כְּתַב to write (perf. כְּתַבוּ, impf. נִכְתֻּב, part. כָּתְבָה(א), כָּתְבָן, pass. כְּתִיב).

כְּתָב (m.) writing (something written), document, (prescribed) limit (E 6:18).

כְּתַל wall (of a building), pl. כֻּתְלַיָּא.

ל

לְ (לַ, etc.) to, for, concerning, of (E 5:11), לְ– "... has;" דִּי לְ–, see דִּי; may also serve to introduce direct objects which are determined (by being in the determinate state, by being proper nouns, by having pronominal suffixes, or by being in cstr. state combinations in which the governed words are determined, e. g. D 2:12, 14, 24). Perhaps the same applies to direct objects quantitatively determined as parts of determined wholes, as in Syriac (cf. C. Brockelmann, *Syrische Grammatik*[4], para. 226), see שְׁטַר. Cf. also לָקֳבֵל, לְמָה, כָּל־קֳבֵל.

לָא (לָה) not (in negative statements and in prohibitions for long periods [E 4:21], other prohibitions taking אַל); כְּלָה as nought, as nothing. See also דִּי לָא.

*לֵב heart, mind, suff. לִבִּי.

לְבַב (m.) intelligence, suff. לִבְבֵהּ "his mind (shall be changed from that of men)."

*לְבוּשׁ raiment, clothing, pl. clothes.

*לְבַשׁ to put on, to wear (impf. יִלְבַּשׁ); *hap̄.* to clothe with (perf. הַלְבִּישׁוּ, for *הַלְבִּשׁוּ).

לֶהֱוֵה, לֶהֱוֹן, לֶהֶוְיָן see הֲוָה.

לָהֵן except, however, but.

*לֵוָי Levite, pl. לֵוָיֵא.

*לְוָת with ("chez"), מִן לְוָתָךְ "from where you are."

לְחֶם (m.) meal, banquet.

*לְחֵנָה concubine.

*לֵילֵא(ה) (*לֵילֵא[ה]) (m.) night, det. לֵילְיָא.

לְמָה lest.

לָקֳבֵל in the presence of, facing, opposite, because of, suff. לָקֳבְלָךְ; דִּי – just as (conj.).

לִשָּׁן (tongue, language, hence) "linguistic community," pl. לִשָּׁנַיָּא.

מ

־מִ, ־מֵ see מִן.

מָא see מָה.

מְאָה hundred, dual מָאתַיִן two hundred, אַרְבַּע מְאָה four hundred.

*מֹאזְנַיִן (dual only) scales, balance, det. מֹאזַנְיָא (for *מֹאזְנַיָּא).

מֵאמַר order, instruction.

מָאן vessel.

מָאתַיִן see מְאָה.

מְגִלָּה (f.) scroll.

מגר *pa.* to overthrow (impf. יְמַגַּר).

*מַדְבַּח altar, det. מַדְבְּחָה.

מִדָּה, מִנְדָּה a kind of tax.

מָדַי Media (< Akk. Madai, P. Māda).

*מָדָיי Mede.

*מְדִינָה province.

*מְדָר, *מְדֹר home.

מָה, מָא what; מָה, מָה דִי whatever. See also כְּמָה, לְמָה.

מוֹת death.

מָזוֹן food, nourishment.

*מְחָא to strike (perf. מְחָת); *pa.* *מַחִי בְּיַד ... to hinder (stop) somebody (impf. יְמַחֵא).

מַחֵא see *חֲיָה.

*מַחְלְקָה division (of the Levites).

מְטָא to arrive, (with ־לְ) to reach, to come to (a thing or a place), (with עַד) — to (a person), (with עַל) to befall (perf. מְטָת, מְטוֹ, impf. יִמְטֵא).

מִישָׁאֵל Mishael.

מֵישַׁךְ Meshach.

*מְלָא to fill (perf. מְלָת, var. מְלָאת, מְלַאת); *hitp.* to be filled with (perf. הִתְמְלִי).

*מַלְאַךְ angel, suff. מַלְאֲכֵהּ.

מִלָּה (f.) word, matter, thing, pl. מִלִּין, etc.

*מְלַח to partake of salt (perf. מְלַחְנָא, but cf. n. to E 4:14).

מְלַח salt.

*מְלֵךְ (m.) advice, counsel, suff. מִלְכִּי.

מֶלֶךְ king; (D 2:44, 47, 7:17) kingdom, kingship, det. מַלְכָּא, pl. מַלְכִין, מַלְכַיָּא (however, in the second sense, prob. voc., according to Ar. *mulk*: *מְלֹךְ, *מָלְכִין, *מָלְכַיָּא).

*מַלְכָּה queen, det. מַלְכְּתָא.

מַלְכוּ (f.) kingdom, kingship, sovereignty, det. מַלְכוּתָה, cstr. מַלְכוּת, suff. מַלְכוּתֵהּ, pl. *מַלְכְוָן, etc.

מלל *pa.* to speak (perf. מַלִּל, part. מְמַלֱּלָה, מְמַלִּל).

מֵמַר see אֲמַר.

מִן (with occasional assimilation of the *n*, as in מִטַּל, מֵאַרְעָא) from, by (the agent of a pass. verb), (more) than, suff. מִנִּי, מִנֵּהּ (D 2:42: "part of it"), מנהון, Q מִנְּהֵין "some of them" (D 2:42), "partly" (D 2:33); מִן דִּי (conj.) after, as soon as, since (causal).

מַן who?; מַן דִּי whoever.

מְנֵא mina (unit of weight or money).

מִנְדָּה see מִדָּה.

מַנְדַּע (m.) mind, intellect, reason (soundness of mind), det. מַנְדְּעָא, suff. מַנְדְּעִי.

מְנָה to count; *pa.* to appoint (perf. מַנִּי, imp. מֱנִּי, E 7:25 "appoint as magistrates and judges, to judge all the population in Transeuphratia, all those who are learned in the laws of your God; and you [pl., i. e. Ezra and his appointees] shall instruct anyone who is not").

מִנְחָה oblation (as a general term, D 2:46), cereal offering (E 7:17).

מִנְיָן number.

*מַעֲבָד doing, deed.

*מְעַיִן (pl. only) belly, suff. מְעוֹהִי.

*מֶעָל (root *ʿll*) going in, pl. מֶעָלֵי שִׁמְשָׁא sunset.

מְפַשַּׁר see *פְּשַׁר.

מָרֵא lord, master, suff. מָרְאִי.

מְרַד rebellion.

*מָרָד, f. מָרָדָא rebellious, det.f. מָרָדְתָּא.

*מְרַט to pluck (*pᵊʿīl* מְרִיטוּ, cf. note to D 7:4).

מֹשֶׁה Moses.

מְשַׁח oil.

*מִשְׁכַּב bed, suff. מִשְׁכְּבִי, etc.

*מִשְׁכַּן dwelling-place, suff. מִשְׁכְּנֵהּ.

*מַשְׁרוֹקִי pipe (musical instrument), det. מַשְׁרֹ(ו)קִיתָא.

מְשָׁרֵא see *שְׁרָה.

*מִשְׁתֵּא see *בֵּי.

*מַתְּנָה (f.) gift.

מַצְלַח success.

נ

נבי (נבא) *hitpa.* to prophesy (perf. הִתְנַבִּי).

*נְבוּאָה prophesying, prophetic guidance.

נְבוּכַדְנֶצַּר Nebuchadnezzar (Akk.).

נִבְזְבָּה gift, pl. נְבָזְבְּיָתָךְ.

*נְבִיא prophet.

*נֶבְרְשָׁה lamp, det. נֶבְרַשְׁתָּא.

*נְגַד to flow (part. נָגֵד, see וְ).

נֶגֶד toward, in the direction of.

*נְגַהּ dawn, det. נָגְהָא.

נְגוֹ see עֲבֵד נְגוֹ.

נדב *hitpa.* to contribute voluntarily (perf. הִתְנַדַּבוּ, part. מִתְנַדַּב, מִתְנַדְּבִין, inf. see *הִתְנַדָּבָה).

נִדְבָּךְ (m.) course, layer of building material in a wall.

נדד to be disturbed, to depart (perf. נַדַּת). Cf. נוד.

*נְדַן sheath, suff. נִדְנֵהּ (see note on D 7:15) (P.).

(אִנְדַּע, etc., see ידע).

*נְהוֹר (m.) light, det. נהירא, Q נְהוֹרָא.

נַהִירוּ understanding.

נְהַר (m.) stream, river.

נוד to go away, to wander, to depart (impf. תְּנֻד, read *תְּנֻּד from נדד ?).

נְוָלוּ, נְוָלִי (miswritten for ־לִי ?) dunghill (Akk. ?).

נוּר (m. and f.) fire, det. נוּרָא.

*נְזִק to be bothered (part. נָזִק); *hap̄.* to trouble, harm (impf. תְּהַנְזִק, part. מְהַנְזְקַת, inf. cstr. הַנְזָקַת [noun of action]).

נְחָשׁ copper.

*נְחִת to descend (part. נָחִת); *hap̄.* to deposit (impf. תַּחֵת, E 6:5 rd. יֵחֹת ?, imp. אֲחֵת, better var. אַחֵת, part. pass. מְהַחֲתִין).

*נְטַל to lift, to carry away (perf. נִטְלֵת); *pᵊʿīl* (מִן אַרְעָא) נְטִילַת "it was annihilated."

*נְטַר to guard (perf. נִטְרֵת).

*נִיחוֹחַ sacrifice of soothing odor, pl. (perhaps alone in use) נִיחֹ(ו)חִין (< H.).

נִכְסִין (pl. only) possessions, property (Akk.).

נְמַר leopard.

נסח *hitp.* to be pulled out (a beam from a building) (impf. יִתְנְסַח).

נסך *pa.* to offer (ritually) (inf. לְנַסָּכָה).

*נְסֵךְ libation, pl. נִסְכֵּיהוֹן (< H.).

(הַסֵּק, הַסִּקוּ, הֻנְסָקָה see סְלִק).

(הַנְעֵל, etc., see עלל).

נְפַל to fall, to be necessary (perf. נפלו [see n. to D 7:20], impf. יִפֵּל, יִפֶּל־ [E 7:20 "that you may have to meet"], תִּפְּלוּן, part. נָפְלִין).

*נְפַק to go (come) out, to issue, to be issued, to appear (D 5:5) (perf. נפקו [see note to D 5:5], imp. פֻּקוּ, part. נָפֵק [see also וְ], נָפְקִין); *hap̄.* to take out, to bring out (perf. הַנְפֵּק, הַנְפִּקוּ).

*נִפְקָה (f.) cost, expenses.

*נִצְבָּה (*נִצְבָה ?) (traditionally) strength; base, element, component (?).

נצח *hitpa.* to distinguish oneself (part. מִתְנַצַּח).

נצל (*h*)*ap̄.* to save, to rescue (part. מַצִּל, inf. לְהַצָּלָה, לְהַצָּלוּתֵהּ).

נְקֵא clean (of fleece, probably of fleece kept covered with a jacket up to the time of shearing).

*נְקַשׁ to knock (intrans.) (part. נָקְשָׁן).

נְשָׂא to take, to carry away (imp. שֵׂא); *hitpa.* to rise up (עַל against) (part. מִתְנַשְּׂאָה).

*נְשִׁין (f.) wives, see *אַנְתָּה.

*נִשְׁמָה breath.

נְשַׁר eagle, vulture, pl. נִשְׁרִין.

*נִשְׁתְּוָן (m.) letter, epistle (P.).

*נְתִין temple servant (H.).

נתן to give (only inf. לְמִנְתַּן and impf. יִנְתֵּן, תִּנְתֵּן, יִנְתְּנוּן, suff. יִתְּנִנֵּהּ, other tenses from יהב).

נתר *ap̄.* to shake off (the leaves of a tree) (imp. אַתַּרוּ).

ס

*סַבַּךְ see *שַׂבַּךְ.

*סְבַר to expect, to intend (impf. יִסְבַּר).

סְגִד to prostrate oneself (impf. יִסְגֻּד, יִסְגְּדוּן, part. סָגְדִין).

*סְגַן prefect, pl. סִגְנִין (Akk.).

*סְגַר to shut (perf. וּסֲגַר).

סובל part. pass. מְסוֹבְלִין laid (foundations) ([Akk.] *s*-conjugation of יבל ?).

סוּמְפֹּנְיָה (סיפניה) musical instrument (bagpipes ?) (Greek *sumphōnia*).

סוף to be fulfilled (perf. סָפַת); *ap̄.* to annihilate (impf. תָּסֵיף).

*סוֹף end.

סיפניה (Q סוּפֹּנְיָה) see סוּמְפֹּנְיָה.

סְלִק to come up, to rise (perf. סִלְקַת [see note to D 7:8], סְלִקוּ, part. סָלְקָן); *hap̄.* to raise (perf. הַסִּקוּ, inf. לְהַנְסָקָה); *hop̄.* to be raised, pulled up (perf. הֻסַּק).

סעד *pa.* to help, to support (לְ– someone) (part. מְסָעֲדִין).

סְפַר (m.) document, book, pl. סִפְרִין, סִפְרַיָּא. See also *דָּכְרָן.

סָפַר scribe, clerk, (E 7:12) scholar, teacher (hardly "[government] secretary for Jewish religious affairs").

*סִפְרָי Sipparite, see *אֲפָרְסָי.

*סַרְבָּל (pl.) trousers (P.).

*סָרַךְ chief minister, pl. סָרְכִין (P.).

סתר *pa.* part. pass. f. pl. מְסַתְּרָתָא things hidden.

*סְתַר to tear down (perf. suff. סַתְרֵהּ).

ע

עֲבַד to make, to do, to act, to commit, to perform (perf. עַבְדֵת, עֲבַדְתְּ, עֲבַ֫דוּ, impf. תַּעַבְדוּן [var. תַּעְבְּדוּן], inf. לְמֶעְבַּד, part. עָבֵד, עָבְדָא, עָבְדִין; *hitp.* pass. (impf. תִּתְעַבְדוּן, יִתְעֲבִד(בֵ)ד, part. מִתְעֲבֵד, מִתְעַבְדָא).

עֲבֵד slave, servant, worshiper, pl. suff. עַבְדָיךְ your servants (respectful for "we, us"), עַבְדוֹ֫הִי.

עֲבֵד נְגוֹ Abed-nego.

*עֲבִידָה (f.) work, administration, service, worship, det. עֲבִידְתָּא.

עֲבַר נַהֲרָא(ה) Transeuphratia (Syria-Palestine) (< Akk.).

עַד until (prep.), idiomatically added in D 7:28 by fusion of the two notions: "thus far the matter" and "here the matter ends." See also דִּבְרַת.

עַד דִּי, עַד (conj.) until, in order that (D 4:22).

*עֲדָה to pass away, to lapse (perf. עֲדָת, impf. יֶעְדֵּה); *hap̄.* to remove, to take away (perf. הֶעְדִּיו, part. מְהַעְדֵּה). In D 3:27, where a Qumran manuscript reads עדה, the context requires the sense of "clung": cf. עדיא, עדיתא (Targum Onkelos to Lev. 13:2ff.) "scab" or the like.

עִדּוֹא Iddo.

עִדָּן (m.) time, season, year.

עוֹד still, yet.

*עֲוָיָה iniquity, misdeed.

עוֹף bird, (collectively) birds.

עוּר chaff.

*עֵז (?) (*ענז ?) (she-)goat, pl. עִזִּין.

*עִזְקָה signet ring.

עֶזְרָא Ezra.

עֲזַרְיָה Azariah.

עֵטָא (root *y'ṭ*) counsel, advice. See also תוב.

עַ֫יִן (f.) eye, cstr. עֵין, pl. עַיְנִין, etc.

עִיר angel (lit. wakeful one, i. e. immortal ?).

עַל on, over (more than), for (in the sense of "because of, on account of"), on behalf of (E 6:17), to (expressing motion toward), against, suff. עֲלַי, עֲלָךְ, עֲלֶ֫ינָא, etc.

עֵ֫לָּא מִן above (prep.).

עִלָּה, עִלָּא ground for accusation.

*עַלְוָה (?) (*עֲלָוָה ?) burnt offering, pl. עֲלָוָן.

*עִלָּי higher, highest, Most High.

*עִלִּי upper chamber, suff. עִלִּיתֵהּ.

*עֶלְיוֹן, pl. קַדִּישֵׁי עֶלְיוֹנִין holy ones of the Most High (a double pl., for logical *קַדִּישֵׁי עֶלְיוֹן).

עלל to go in, to come in (perf. עַל, עללת, Q עַלַּת, part. עללין, Q עָלִּין); *hap̄*. to bring in, to take in (perf. הַנְעֵל, imp. suff. הַעֵלְנִי, inf. לְהַנְעָלָה, לְהֶעָלָה); *hop̄*. to be brought (taken) in (perf. הֻעַל, הֻעַלוּ). See also *מֶעָל.

עָלַם eternity, the remote past or the remote future, det. עָלְמָא, pl. עָלְמִין, עָלְמַיָּא; לְעָלַם, לְעָלְמִין forever, מִן יוֹמָת עָלְמָא since the days of old, from earliest times.

*עֵלְמָי Elamite.

*עֲלַע (f.) rib, pl. עִלְעִין (D 7:5, conjectural emendation *תָּלְעָן "fangs" [H. מְתַלְּעוֹת]).

עַם people, folk, det. עַמָּא, pl. עַמְמַיָּא.

עִם (along, together) with, (D 5:21) like, (D 3:33, 4:31, 7:2) in (temporal), (E 6:8, D 3:32) for, suff. עִמִּי, עִמָּךְ, etc.

*עַמִּיק deep, pl. f. עַמִּיקָתָא deep, hidden things.

עֲמַר (m.) fleece.

*עַןְ, *עֶנֶת, *עֶת see כְּעַן, etc.

*עֲנָה to speak up, to respond, to reply (perf. עֲנָת, עֲנוֹ, part. עָנֵה, עָנַיִן).

*עֲנֵה poor, wretched, pl. (in pause) עֲנָיִן.

*עֲנָן cloud.

*עֲנַף branch, pl. עַנְפוֹהִי.

עֲנָשׁ fine, compensation.

*עֳפִי (m.) foliage, suff. עָפְיֵהּ.

עֲצִיב sad.

עקר *itp*. to be uprooted (אתעקרו, see n. to D 7:8).

עִקַּר stock, trunk (of a tree), שָׁרְשׁוֹהִי – its root-trunk.

*עַר adversary, pl. עָרָיךְ.

ערב *pa*. part. pass. מְעָרַב mixed; *hitpa*. part. מִתְעָרַב, מִתְעָרְבִין mixing (intrans.).

*עֲרָד wild ass, onager.

*עַרְוָה nakedness, shame.

עֲשַׂב herb(age), grass, det. עִשְׂבָּא.

עַשְׂרָה, f. עֲשַׂר ten.

עֶשְׂרִין twenty.

עֲשִׁית pleased, graciously inclined.

*עֲתִיד prepared, ready.

עַתִּיק old, ancient.

פ

פֶּחָה governor, cstr. פַּחַת, pl. פַּחֲוָתָא (Akk.).

פֶּחָר potter.

*פַּטִישׁ shirt (?), pl. פַּטְישֵׁיהוֹן (hardly *פְּטַשׁ < Greek *petasos*, with either פ׳ or כַּרְבְּלָתְהוֹן a gloss).

*פְּלַג to divide (part. pass. פְּלִיגָה).

פְּלַג half.

*פְּלֻגָּה class (of priests).

פְּלַח to worship (impf. יִפְלְחוּן, part. פָּלַח, פָּלְחִין, פָּלְחֵי [with לְ- except D 3:17]).

פָּלְחָן worship, (divine) service, cult.

פֻּם (m.) mouth, opening, suff. פֻּמַּהּ.

פַּס (m.) palm (פַּס יְדָה, פַּסָּא דִי יְדָא [D 5:5, 24] simply "the hand," used instead of the simple יְדָא in order to exclude the arm).

פְּסַנְתֵּרִין (פְּסַנְטֵרִין) psaltery (Greek *psaltērin* < *psaltērion*).

פַּרְזֶל (m.) iron, det. פַּרְזְלָא.

פרס $p^{e}{}^{c}\bar{\imath}l$ to be broken off (פְּרִיסַת).

פְּרֵס half-mina (unit of weight or money), pl. פַּרְסִין.

פָּרַס, in pause פָּרָס Persia (P.).

*פַּרְסָי Persian.

*פְּרַק to atone for, to redeem (imp. פְּרֻק).

פרשׁ *pa.* part. pass. מְפָרַשׁ accurately (or, in translation ?).

פַּרְשֶׁגֶן (m.) copy (P.).

*פְּשַׁר to interpret (inf. לְמִפְשַׁר); *pa.* part. מְפַשַּׁר (D 5:12) "an interpreter" (but prob. read מִפְשַׁר "interpreting" [$p^{e}{}^{c}al$ noun of action]).

פְּשַׁר interpretation, det. פִּשְׁרָא, etc.

פִּתְגָם (m.) message, word, matter (P.).

*פְּתַח to open (part. pass. פְּתִיחָן); $p^{e}{}^{c}\bar{\imath}l$ passive (פְּתִיחוּ).

*פְּתָי width, breadth.

צ

*צְבִי to want, to wish (perf. צְבִית, impf. יִצְבֵּא, inf. suff. כְּמִצְבְּיֵהּ).

צְבוּ (f.) thing, matter.

צבע *pa.* to drench (part. מְצַבְּעִין); *hitpa.* to be drenched (impf. יִצְטַבַּע).

*צַד aspect, לְצַד against, מִצַּד as regards.

*צְדָא see הַצְדָא.

צִדְקָה charity.

*צַוַּאר neck, suff. צַוְּארֵהּ.

צלי *pa.* to pray (part. מְצַלֵּא[לְּא], מְצַלַּיִן).

צלח *hap̄.* to promote, to fare well, to prosper (perf. הַצְלַח, part. מַצְלְחִין). See also מַצְלַח.

צְלֵם (m.) statue, det. צַלְמָא.

צְלֵם complexion.

*צְפִיר, pl. צְפִירֵי עִזִּין (male) goats (E 6:17). Cf. n. to D 4:30.

*צִפַּר (f.) bird, pl. צִפְּרִין, etc.

ק

קבל *pa.* to receive, to take over (perf. קַבֵּל, impf. יְקַבְּלוּן).

קֳבֵל see כָּל־קֳבֵל and לָקֳבֵל.

קַדִּישׁ holy being (D 4:10,14,20), (prob.) saint (D 7:18, 21, 22, 25), (adj.) holy (D 4:5, 6, 15, 5:11).

קֳדָם (prep.) before, in the presence of (substituted for "to" in connection with words addressed to God or king), suff. קֳדָמַי (in pause קֳדָמָי) or קֳדָמַי, קֳדָמָיךְ, etc.

*קַדְמָי first, former, f. det. קַדְמָיְתָא, pl. קַדְמָיֵא, קַדְמָיָתָא.

קַדְמַת in דְּנָה (מִקַּדְמַת) מִן – formerly.

קום to arise, to stand, to endure, to attend (קֳדָם on) (perf. קָם, קָמוּ, impf. יְקוּם, יְקוּמוּן, imp. קוּמִי, part. קָאֵם, קאמין, Q קָיְמִין, קָאֲמַיָּא); *pa.* to decree (inf. לְקַיָּמָה); *hap̄.* to erect, to install, to appoint, to decree (perf. הֲקֵים, וַהֲקֵים, הֲקֵימְתָּ, הֲקֵימֶת, הֲקִימוּ, suff. הֲקִימֵהּ, אֲקִימֵהּ, impf. יְקִים, יְהָקֵים, תְּקִים, inf. suff. לַהֲקָמוּתֵהּ, part. מְהָקֵים); *hop̄.* to be set up, raised (perf. הֳקִימַת, הֳקָמַת).

*קְטַל to kill (a small number of victims) (part. קָטֵל); *pᵊʿīl* passive (קְטִיל, קְטִילַת); *hitp.* to be killed (of a small number of victims) (inf. לְהִתְקְטָלָה); *pa.* to kill (a large number of victims) (perf. קַטִּל); *hitpa.* to be killed (of a large number of victims) (part. מִתְקַטְּלִין).

*קְטַר (m.) knot, joint, pl. קִטְרִין.

קַיִט summer.

קְיָם decree.

קַיָּם, f. קַיָּמָה enduring.

קיתרוס (Q קַתְרוֹס) zither (Greek *kitharis*).

קָל (m.) voice.

*קְנָה to purchase (impf. תִּקְנֵא).

קְצַף to be(come) angry.

קְצַף anger.

קצץ *pa.* to lop off (imp. קַצִּצוּ).

קְצָת (approximately: sum, measure) in מִן – part of, לִקְצָת after the lapse of, at the end of (a period of time).

*קְרָא to cry, to shout, to read (impf. יִקְרֵה, אֶקְרֵא, יִקְרוֹן, part. קָרֵא, inf. לְמִקְרֵא); *pᵊʿīl* to be read (קֱרִי); *hitp.* to be called, designated as (impf. יִתְקְרֵי).

קְרֵב to approach, to walk over to (עַל a person, לְ– a thing) (perf. קִרְבַת, קְרִבוּ, inf. suff. כְּמִקְרְבֵהּ); *pa.* to offer (ritually) (impf. תְּקָרֵב);

hap̄. to admit (קֳדָם into the presence of), to offer (ritually) (perf. הַקְרִבוּ, suff. הַקְרְבוּהִי, part. מְהַקְרְבִין).

קְרָב war, battle.

קִרְיָא (f.) city, det. קִרְיְתָא, pl. *קֳרֵא (cf. Ar. and Syr.), det. (conjectural) *קָרְיָהּ (or suff. *קָרְיַהּ), for קִרְיָה, E 4:10.

קֶרֶן (f.) horn (of animals, also a musical instrument), det. קַרְנָא, dual קַרְנַיִן, det. קַרְנַיָּא.

*קְרַץ piece, אֲכַלוּ קַרְצֵיהוֹן דִּי "they denounced (the Jews)."

קְשֹׁט faithfulness, – מִן of a truth, truly, unquestionably.

ר

רֵאשׁ head, (D 7:1) רֵאשׁ מִלִּין אֲמַר "he began his account thus" (cf. v. 28), pl. רֵאשִׁין, suff. רָאשֵׁיהֹם (Hebraism?).

רַב great, big, det. רַבָּא, f. רַבְּתָא, pl. רַבְרְבִין, f. רַבְרְבָן, רַבְרְבָתָא; (noun) captain, commander, chief, pl. *רַבְרְבָנִין, רַבְרְבָנֵי, etc. magnates, nobles.

רְבָה to grow, to wax great (perf. רְבָת, רבית, Q רְבַת D 4:19); *pa.* to advance, to promote (perf. רַבִּי).

רִבּוֹ myriad, ten thousand, pl. רבון (see note to D 7:10).

*רְבִיעָי, f. רביעיא(ה), Q רְבִיעָאָה fourth, det. רְבִיעָיְתָא.

רגז *hap̄.* to anger, to provoke (perf. הַרְגִּזוּ).

רְגַז anger, wrath.

*רְגַל (*רֶגֶל?) (f.) leg, foot, dual רַגְלַיִן, רַגְלַיָּא, etc.

רגשׁ *hap̄.* to go (come) in a body to (עַל) somebody (perf. הַרְגִּשׁוּ).

*רֵו (m.) appearance.

רוּחַ (f.; m. D 2:35) wind, spirit.

רום to be(come) haughty (perf. רִם); *hap̄.* to exalt (part. מָרִים); *pōlel* *רוֹמֵם to exalt (part. מְרוֹמֵם); *hitpōlal* to exalt oneself (perf. הִתְרוֹמַמְתָּ).

*רוּם (m.) height.

רָז (m.) secret, mystery (P.).

רְחוּם Rehum.

*רַחִיק distant.

רַחֲמִין (pl. only) mercy.

רחץ *hitp.* to trust (עַל in) (perf. הִתְרְחִצוּ).

רֵיחַ smell.

*רְמָה to cast, to impose (taxes) (perf. רְמוֹ, רְמֵינָא, inf. לְמִרְמֵא); *pᵉʿīl* to be cast, to be set up (a throne) (רְמִיו); *hitp.* to be cast (impf. יִתְרְמֵא, תִּתְרְמֵא).

*רְעוּ wish, pleasure, cstr. רְעוּת.

*רַעְיוֹן (m.) thought.

רַעְנַן vigorous, healthy.

רעע to break (impf. תֵּרֹעַ); *pa.* to break, to smash (part. מְרָעַע).

*רְפַס to trample (part. רָפְסָה).

רְשַׁם to draw up, to write down, to record (perf. רְשַׁמְתָּ, impf. תִּרְשֻׁם); *pəʿīl* passive (רְשִׁים).

שׂ

*שָׂב elder.

*שַׂבְּךְ (*סַבְּךְ) trigon (a musical instrument), det. שַׂ(ס)בְּכָא.

*שְׂגָא (?) (*שְׂגִי ?) to increase (intrans.), to be much (impf. יִשְׂגֵּא).

שַׂגִּיא much, great, (adv.) very, exceedingly, pl. many.

*שָׂהֲדוּ testimony, det. שָׂהֲדוּתָא.

שְׂטַר (m.) side, end, D 7:5 (see note) "and it raised one end (i.e., its front end) upright" (שְׂטַר חַד being quantitatively determined, for חַד מִן שִׂטְרַיהּ, cf. לְ above).

שִׂים to set, to place, to appoint, בָּל – to set one's mind, ... שֻׁם – to name (somebody) (perf. שָׂם, שָׂמְתָּ, שָׂמֶת, שָׂמוּ, suff. שָׂמֵהּ, imp. שִׂימוּ); *pəʿīl* passive (שִׂים, שֻׂמַת); *hiṯp.* (*hittap̄.* ?) passive (impf. יִתְּשָׂמוּן, part. מִתְּשָׂם).

שׂכל *hiṯpa.* to observe, to watch (בְּ– direct object) (part. מִשְׂתַּכַּל).

שָׂכְלְתָנוּ intelligence.

*שָׂנֵא enemy, pl. שָׂנְאָךְ.

שְׂעַר (m.) hair (coll.), suff. שַׂעְרֵהּ.

שׁ

שְׁאֵל to ask somebody (לְ– or direct object) for something (direct object) (perf. שְׁאֵלְנָא, impf. יִשְׁאֲלֶנְכוֹן, part. שָׁאֵל).

*שְׁאֵלָה matter, requirement, det. שְׁאֵלְתָא.

שְׁאַלְתִּיאֵל Shealtiel.

שְׁאָר (cstr.) "the rest of," "the other (pl.)."

שׁבח *pa.* to praise, to give praise (perf. שַׁבַּח, שַׁבַּחְתָּ, שַׁבְּחֵת, שַׁבַּחוּ, part. מְשַׁבַּח).

*שְׁבַט (m.) tribe, pl. שִׁבְטֵי.

*שְׁבִיב (m.) flame, tongue (of fire).

שִׁבְעָה (f. *שְׁבַע) seven, cstr. (before a det. noun) שִׁבְעַת, חַד שִׁבְעָה seven times (as much or more).

*שְׁבַק to leave, to let be (imp. שְׁבֻקוּ, inf. לְמִשְׁבַּק); *hiṯp.* to be left (impf. תִּשְׁתְּבִק).

שׁבשׁ *hiṯpa.* part. pl. מִשְׁתַּבְּשִׁין bewildered.

*שֵׁגַל king's wife, pl. שֵׁגְלָתֵהּ.

שׁדר *hiṯpa.* to strive, to exert oneself (part. מִשְׁתַּדַּר).

שַׁדְרַךְ Shadrach.

שׁוי *pa.* to make like (עִם) (perf. שׁוי, Q שַׁוִּיו); *hitpa.* to be turned into (impf. יִשְׁתַּוֵּה).

*שׁוּר (m.) wall (of a city).

*שׁוּשַׁנְכָי Susian, of Susa (Shushan), pl. שׁוּשַׁנְכָיֵא (P.).

*שְׁחִית, f. שְׁחִיתָה corrupt, vicious, wicked.

שְׁחִיתָה (f.) fault, corruption.

שֵׁיזִב ([Akk.] š-conjugation of ʿzb) to save, to deliver, to succor (impf. יְשֵׁיזִב, suff. יְשֵׁיזְבִנְכוֹן, יְשֵׁיזְבִנָךְ, part. מְשֵׁיזִב, inf. suff. לְשֵׁיזָבוּתֵהּ, ־תָךְ, ־תַנָא).

שֵׁיצִיא ([Akk.] š-conjugation of yṣʾ) to complete (E 6:15, prob. read pl. שֵׁיצִיו).

שׁכח *hitp.* to be found (perf. הִשְׁתְּכַח, הִשְׁתְּכַחַת, הִשְׁתְּכַחַתְּ); *hap̄.* to find, to obtain (perf. הַשְׁכַּחוּ, הַשְׁכַּחְנָא, impf. תְּהַשְׁכַּח, נְהַשְׁכַּח, inf. לְהַשְׁכָּחָה).

*שׁכלל ([Akk.] š-conjugation of *kll*) to complete (perf. שַׁכְלִלוּ, suff. שַׁכְלְלֵהּ, inf. לְשַׁכְלָלָה); *hitpa.* to be completed (impf. יִשְׁתַּכְלְלוּן).

שׁכן to dwell, to perch (of birds) (impf. יִשְׁכְּנָן); *pa.* to make ... dwell (perf. שַׁכִּן).

שְׁלֵה secure, carefree, happy.

שׁלה see שָׁלוּ.

שָׁלוּ (f.) treachery, guile (in D 3:29, K שׁלה).

*שְׁלֵוָה happiness, suff. שְׁלֵוְתָךְ.

שְׁלַח to send, to send word, יַד ־ to raise a (hostile) hand (perf. שְׁלַחוּ, שְׁלַחְנָא, שְׁלַחְתּוּן, impf. יִשְׁלַח); *p*ᵊʿ*īl* שְׁלִיחַ, E 7:14 [impersonal] "a mission has been dispatched" (unless שְׁלִיחַ is pass. part. and "you" has to be supplied: "you are commissioned").

שְׁלֵט to rule, to have power over, to overpower (all with בְּ־) (perf. שְׁלִטוּ, impf. יִשְׁלַט, תִּשְׁלַט); *hap̄.* to give power, dominion (בְּ־ over) (perf. suff. הַשְׁלְטֵהּ, הַשְׁלְטָךְ).

*שִׁלְטֹן official.

שָׁלְטָן (m.) ruler, power, dominion, government.

שַׁלִּיט (with בְּ־) in control of, having dominion over, (with לְ־) lawful to; (noun) high official.

שְׁלִם to be finished; *hap̄.* to hand over, to deliver (perf. suff. הַשְׁלְמֵהּ, impf. הַשְׁלֵם).

שְׁלָם (m.) well-being, greetings!

שֻׁם name, לְשֵׁשְׁבַּצַּר שְׁמֵהּ "to a certain Sheshbazzar," pl. שְׁמָהָת, שְׁמָהָתְהֹם.

שׁמד *hap̄.* to annihilate (inf. לְהַשְׁמָדָה).

*שְׁמַיִן (m.) (pl. only) heaven, sky (D 4:23: Heaven, i.e., God), det. שְׁמַיָּא.

שׁמם *iṯpōlal* אֶשְׁתּוֹמַם to stare, to be dazed.

שְׁמַע to hear (perf. שִׁמְעֵת, impf. יִשְׁמַע, תִּשְׁמַע, תִּשְׁמְעוּן, part. שָׁמְעִין); *hiṯpa.* to obey, to owe allegiance (-לְ to) (impf. יִשְׁתַּמְּעוּן).

*שָׁמְרַיִן (in pause שָׁמְרָיִן) Samaria (city and province).

שׁמשׁ *pa.* to serve (impf. suff. יְשַׁמְּשׁוּנֵּהּ).

*שְׁמַשׁ sun, det. שִׁמְשָׁא.

שִׁמְשַׁי Shimshai.

*שֵׁן (f.) tooth, dual (for pl.) שִׁנַּיִן, שִׁנַּיהּ.

*שְׁנָה (f.) year, cstr. שְׁנַת, pl. שְׁנִין.

*שְׁנָה (*שֵׁנָה ?) (f.) sleep, suff. שִׁנְתֵּהּ.

*שְׁנָה to be (become) different, to be done contrary to orders, to change color (of the face) (perf. שְׁנוֹ, suff. שְׁנוֹהִי, impf. יִשְׁנֵא, תִּשְׁנֵא, part. שָׁנְיָה, שָׁנְיָן, שָׁנַיִן); *pa.* to transform, to alter (trans.), to disobey (an order) (perf. שַׁנִּיו, impf. יְשַׁנּוֹן, part. pass. מְשַׁנְּיָה "different in character"); *iṯpa.* to change (intrans.), to change color (of the face) (perf. אשתנו, Q אֶשְׁתַּנִּי, impf. יִשְׁתַּנּוֹן, jussive יִשְׁתַּנּוֹ); *hap̄.* to change (trans.), to transgress (part. מְהַשְׁנֵא, inf. לְהַשְׁנָיָה).

שָׁעָה (f.) hour, while, det. בַּהּ שַׁעֲתָא (var. שָׁעֲתָא) at that moment, forthwith.

*שָׁפֵט magistrate, pl. שָׁפְטִין (H. ?).

שַׁפִּיר beautiful.

שׁפל *hap̄.* to bring low, to abase, to humble (perf. הַשְׁפֵּלְתְּ, impf. יְהַשְׁפִּל, part. מַשְׁפִּיל, inf. לְהַשְׁפָּלָה).

שְׁפַל lowly, humble.

שְׁפַר to be pleasing (impf. יִשְׁפַּר).

*שְׁפַרְפָּר dawn.

*שָׁק thigh.

*שְׁרָה to loosen, to untie (inf. לְמִשְׁרֵא, part. pass. שְׁרֵא, שְׁרַיִן loose, residing); *pa.* to begin (perf. שָׁרִיו), part. מְשָׁרֵא (D 5:12) "one who loosens" (but prob. read מִשְׁרֵא "untying" [*pəʿal* noun of action]); *hiṯpa.* to become loose (part. מִשְׁתָּרַיִן).

*שְׁרֹשׁ root, pl. שָׁרְשׁוֹהִי.

שרשו (Q שְׁרֹשִׁי) corporal punishment (P.).

שֵׁשְׁבַּצַּר Sheshbazzar (Akk.).

שֵׁת (שִׁת) (f.) six.

שִׁתִּין sixty.

שׁתי see אִשְׁתִּי.

שְׁתַר בּוֹזְנַי Shethar-bozenai (P.).

ת

*תְּבַר to break (part. pass. תְּבִירָה).

*תְּדִיר in בִּתְדִירָא constantly.

תוב to come back, to return (intrans.) (impf. יְתוּב); *hap̄.* to return (trans.), to send back, פִּתְגָם – to reply (with the person as a second direct object), עֵטָא וּטְעֵם לְ– – D 2:14 "took counsel with (Arioch)" (perf. הֲתִיב, suff. הֲתִיבוּנָא, impf. יְתִיבוּן, יַהֲתִיבוּן, inf. suff. לַהֲתָבוּתָךְ).

תְּוַהּ to be startled.

*תּוֹר ox (as a general term, German "Rind"), bull, pl. תּוֹרִין cattle, bulls, בְּנֵי תוֹרִין oxen, cattle.

תְּחוֹת, *תַּחַת under (prep.), suff. תְּחֹתוֹהִי, but with מִן: מִן תַּחְתּוֹהִי, תְּחוֹת כָּל־ שְׁמַיָּא everywhere under heaven.

תְּלַג (m.) snow.

*תְּלִיתָי, f. תליתיא, Q תְּלִיתָאָה third.

תַּלְתָּא, תַּלְתִּי triumvir.

תְּלָתָה(א), f. תְּלָת, three, תְּלָתֵיהוֹן the three of them.

תְּלָתִין thirty.

תַּמָּה there.

*תְּמַהּ (m.) wonder, miracle, pl. תִּמְהִין.

*תִּנְיָן, f. תִּנְיָנָה second.

תִּנְיָנוּת (adv.) a second time.

*תִּפְתָּי (?) chief of police, pl. תִּפְתָּיֵא.

*תַּקִּיף, f. תַּקִּיפָה(א) strong, powerful.

*תְּקַל *pəʿīl* to be weighed (תְּקִילְתָּה).

תְּקֵל shekel (unit of weight or money).

תקן *hop̄.* to be reinstated (perf. הָתְקְנַת).

תְּקִף to wax mighty (perf. תְּקֵפַת, תִּקְפַת); *pa.* to strengthen, to issue a strong (prohibition) (inf. לְתַקָּפָה).

תְּקָף might, power, det. תָּקְפָּא.

*תְּרֵין, f. תַּרְתֵּין, two, cstr. תְּרֵי עֲשַׂר twelve (m.).

תְּרַע gate, royal court.

*תָּרָע gatekeeper.

תַּרְתֵּין see *תְּרֵין.

תַּתְּנַי Tattenai (Akk.).

IV. PALMYRENE-HATRAN-NABATAEAN

(Harald Ingholt)

(Pa., Ha., and Na. respectively indicate whether an entry refers to the Palmyrene, Hatran, or Nabatean texts. The fact that the three dialects are grouped here together is, of course, not meant to prejudge their dialectal relationship in any way.

Names are easily recognizable by the capital letter with which they begin. Unless otherwise specified, they are male personal names. Wherever the proper vocalization is considered uncertain, it has been given in brackets. However, even where the vocalization is fixed by Greek and other transcriptions or by the etymology, it has been considered impractical here to adopt a strictly uniform and consistent rendering in Latin characters.)

ʾ

ʾb Ab (= August) (Pa.).
ʾb father (suff. *ʾbwhy*) (Na.).
ʾbʾ (Abbā) (Ha.).
ʾbw (f.) (Abū) (Ha.).
ʾgr *ap̄.* to rent (impf. *ywgr*) (Na.); *ʾgwr* contractor; **ʾgrʾ* (det. *ʾgryʾ*, *ʾgwryʾ*) contract (Pa.).
ʾgrpʾ Agrippa (Pa.).
ʾgtpws Agathopūs (Pa.).
ʾdʾ (Addā) (Pa., Ha.).
ʾdy (Adday) (Ha.).
ʾdynt Odaynath (Pa.).
ʾdr Adar (= March) (Pa., Ha.).
ʾdrwn cella (Pa.).
ʾw or (Na.), *ʾw* . . . *ʾw* either . . . or (Pa.).
ʾwrlyʾ (f.) Aurelia; (Pa. 11^{5}) (m.) *Aurelie* = Aurelius (Pa).
ʾwrlys Aurelius (Pa.).
ʾḥ brother (sg. or pl. suff. m. *ʾḥwhy*, pl. suff. f. *ʾḥyh*) (Ha., Na.).
ʾḥd to occupy (a tomb) (Na.), to take property (= to be settled) (Ha. 20^{7}).
ʾḥr offspring, posterity (Na.).
ʾydʿn (Aydaʿān) (Pa.).
ʾyšw (Iyāšū) (Na.).
ʾyty there is (shall be) (Na.).
ʾytybl ʾAythībēl (Na.).
ʾksdrʾ exedra (ἐξέδρα) (Pa.).
(*ʾl* Ar. definite article.)
ʾlgšyʾ Vologesias (place name).
ʾlh god (pl. det. *ʾlhyʾ*, *ʾlhʾ*) (Pa., Ha., Na.).
ʾlh these (Na.). See also *ʾln*, *ʾnw*.
ʾlḥgrw El-Ḥejrā (place name) (Na.).
ʾlwl Elūl (= September) (Pa., Ha.).
ʾlkw$^{d}/_{r}$ (Elkūr?) (Ha.).
ʾlksdrs, *ʾlksndrws* Alexander (Pa.).
ʾlksy (Elkasī) (Na.).
ʾln these (Pa.). See also *ʾlh*, *ʾnw*.
ʾlʿzʾ Al-ʿUzzā (f. deity) (Na.).
ʾlp thousand (Na.).
ʾlp *eṯpa.* to compose (a document) (impf. *ytʾlp*) (Na.).
ʾlqbrw see *qbr*.
ʾlt (Na. 9^{5} *ʾltw*) Allāt (f. deity).
ʾm mother (Ha., Na.).
ʾmdbw (f.) Emdabū (Pa.).
ʾmyt (f.) Umayyath (Na.).
ʾmn craftsman, architect, sculptor (Na.).
ʾmr to say, to appoint (perf. *ʾmrt*: "whom Ašurbēl has named 'daughter of God'"?) (Ha.).
ʾn if (Pa.). See also *hn*.
ʾnw these (Na.).
ʾnwš see *ʾnš*.
ʾnynws (Anīnōs, Annianus?) (Pa.).
ʾnš (Pa., Ha.), *ʾnwš* (Na.) anybody, (coll.) men, people, *ʾnwš klh* anybody, *lʾ* . . . *ʾnwš klh*, *lʾ* . . . *ʾnš* nobody.

ʾntʾ, ʾttʾ wife (cstr. *ʾntt*, suff. *ʾntth, ʾtth*) (Pa., Ha., Na.).
ʾsṭrṭg (Pa.), *ʾsrtg* (Na.) commander (στρατηγός).
(*ʾsq, ʾsqw* see *slq*.)
ʾsr see *rb*.
ʾsrtgʾ see *ʾsṭrṭg*.
ʾstnq (Parthian [?] proper name) (Ha.).
ʾp also (Pa.).
ʾpkʾ Efca (place name).
ʾpkl priest, *rb ʾpkl* chief priest (Ha., Na.).
ʾprhṭ Afrahaṭ (Pa.).
ʾptḥ (Aftaḥ) (Na.).
ʾṣdq b ʾṣdq each legal kinsman (Na.).
ʾṣl some architectural term (Na.).
ʾqyḥ (ʾAqqīḥ) (Pa.).
ʾrbʿyn forty (Na.).
ʾrdkl architect (Ha.).
ʾrkwn archon (ἄρχων) (Pa.).
ʾrn box (reading uncertain) (Pa.).
ʾrsksh (f.) (Arioxe) (Na.).
ʾrṣw Arṣū (deity) (Pa.).
ʾrʿ see *rʿ*.
ʾšʾ (Ašā) (Ha.).
(*ʾšr* see *šrr*.)
ʾšrbl (Ašurbēl) (deity) (Ha.).
ʾšrw Ašar (deity) (Na.).
ʾšṭṭy (Aštaṭay) (Ha.).
ʾtʾ *ap̄*. to bring (perf. *ʾyty, ʾty*) (Pa.) See also *mytwytʾ*.
ʾtlw (Atalū) (Ha.).
ʾtr place, base (Pa., Na.).
ʾtʿqb Atēʿaqab (Pa.).
ʾtrʿtʾ Atargatis (f. deity) (Ha.).
ʾttʾ see *ʾntʾ*.

B

b in, at, on, during, (together) with, through (= by right of Ha. $20^{9\text{-}10}$), distributive (see *ʾṣdq*), suff. *bh, bhm* (Pa., Ha., Na.).
b (< *byt*) see *yld*.
bʾr cistern (pl. cstr. *bʾrwt*) (Na.).
bb gate (Pa.).
bbl Babel (place name) (Pa.)
bgn invocation (*ʿl* "in favor of" or "against") (Ha.).
bdyl dy because (conj.); *bdyl kwt* that is why (Pa.).
bwlʾ senate (βουλή) (Pa.).
bwlḥʾ Bōlḥā (Pa.).
bwly Bōlay (Pa.).
bwnʾ Bōnnā (Pa.).
bwšʾ Būšā (Ha. 11^3 ʿAbdil Būšā, or rather: Lābōšā has made).
bṭl *pa.* to concern (*mbṭl* it concerns) (Pa.).
byldʾ see *yld*.
byn *ap̄*. to make known (impf. *ybnwn*) (Pa.).
byny between (Pa. 11^9 *bnyhwn*), *byny . . . lbyny* between . . . and (Pa.).
byt, bt house, structure, temple (pl. *bty, btyʾ*), *bty mqbryn* burial places, *byt šlṭwn* territory of jurisdiction. See also *dwd, yld, mrʾ, *nḥrʾ, nṭr, ʿqbʾ, tkdm* (Pa., Ha., Na.).
bl Bēl (deity), or Lord (Pa., Ha.).
blgʾ (Bēlgā) (Ha.).
blḥd only (Na.).
blʿd except (Na.).
bnʾ, bnh to build; *bnʾ* (det. *bnyh*) builder; *bnyn* building (Pa., Ha., Na.).
bny see *byny, br*.
bnt see *br*.
bʿl husband (Ha.); *bʿlšm(y)n, bʿšmyn* Baʿal Šamīn "Lord of Heaven" (deity) (Ha.).
br son, child (pl. cstr. *bny, bnʾ* [often in tribal names], suff. *bnwhy, bnwh, bnyhy, bnyhm, bnyhwn, bnyhn*), *bnʾ byt* members of a household; *br* is sometimes omitted in Pa. pedigrees (Pa., Ha., Na.); *brʾ* daughter (cstr. *brt, bt*, suff. *brth*, pl. cstr. *bnt*, suff. *bnth*), *brt šnt . . .* ". . . years old" (Pa., Ha., Na.). See also *dd, dkʾ, zby, ḥry, mdkʾ, smy*.
br in *lbr* outside, abroad (Ha.).
brmryn Bar Mārayn (deity, or referring to the heir-apparent) (Ha.).
brʾ (Berā) (Ha.).
bry outer (pl. *bryyn*) (Pa.).
bryk blessed (Pa., Ha.); *bryk šmh lʿlmʾ* (deity) whose name be blessed forever (Pa.).
brytʾ (f. det.) exorcizer (Ha.).
brnny Bar Nanay (Ha.).
brsmyʾ Bar Šamayyâ (= Heaven, Bar Semayâ = Standard?) (Pa.).
brʿth Barʿatē (Pa.).

brš'd' Baršo'adâ (Pa.).
brt see *br*.
bt see *byt*, *br*. See also *zby*, *prmwn*, *smy*.
bt 'qb' Bēṯ 'Aqbā (place name) (Ha.)
btr beyond (prep.) (Pa.).

G

gb' to collect, levy (taxes); *etp*. to be taxed (part. *mtgbyn*) (Pa.).
gblw (Gabalū) (Ha.).
gd (Pa.), *gnd* (also *gd*) (Ha.) Gad (deity), god, Fortune, divine glory (of kings). See also *'m*.
gdy' Gadyā [Ha.].
gdybwl Gaddībōl (tribal name) (Pa.).
gw in *lgw* inside, at home (Ha.), *lgw mn* inside (prep.) (Pa.), *gw' mn* inside (prep.) (Na.).
gwmḥ (Pa.), *gwḥ* (Na.) niche.
gwp corpse (Ha.).
gzzt' (f. det.) treasurer (?, or rather a kind of religious functionary, from the root *gzz*).
gzy't Guzay'ath (Na.).
gy'' Gaia (place name) (Na.).
gll stele (Pa.).
glp to sculpture; *glp* sculptor (Pa., Ha.).
gn' garden (cstr. *gnt*, pl. *gny'*) (Pa., Na.: "couch" [?]). See also *smk*.
gnd see *gd*.
gns manner (Pa.).
grymy (Goraymay) (Pa.).
grmṭws secretary (γραμματεύς), *grmṭy'* secretaryship (γραμματεία) (Pa.).
gt corpse (Na.).

D

d see *dy*.
d' this (m.) (Na. < Ar.); this (f.), see *dnh*.
d'klh (Parthian[?] f. proper name) (Ha.).
dbr to lead (Pa.; Ha. impf. *ldbr hnw bqṭyr'* will drive them out by force).
d/rbš meaning uncertain (Ha.).
dgm' decree (δόγμα) (Pa.).
dd in *bn' ddhwn* (Ha.) their cousins (or *bn' dr-* their contemporaries).
dh see *dnh*.
dwd cauldron, *bt dwd'* (pl. det.) kitchen (Pa.).
dwmt' Dūmtā (place name) (Na.).
dwšpry (Iranian proper name) (Ha.).
dwšr' Dūšarā (deity) (Na.).
dy, *d* who, which, of (gen.), (Na. no. 7[1]) that which; (conj.) (so) that, because, (Pa. 9[5]: *d*) namely that, *mn dy* because (Pa., Ha. [*dy*, *d*], Na. [*dy*]). See also *bdyl*, *dyd-*, *dyl-*, *kd*, *kdy*, *mh*, *mn*.
dyd- (Pa.), *dyl-* (Ha.) independent possessive pronoun (*dydh*, *dylhwn* "[the temple] belonging to them [for which they rejoice]").
dk' (consecrated) place (det. *dkt'*, Pa. 19[2] *br dkt'* "son of the [consecrated] place [of the chamber]," referring to the offspring of a hierogamia) (Pa.).
dkr to remember, to mention (impf. suff. *ldkrhy* [Ha.], part. pass. *dkyr*, *dkyryn*, *dkyr⟨y⟩n*) (Pa., Ha., Na.); *dkrn* memory (Pa.).
dkr male (children) (Na.).
dmws, *dms* people (δῆμος) (Pa.).
dmsps Damasippos (Na.).
dnh this (m.), *dh* (Pa.), *d'* (Na.) this (f.).

H

hblw Hubal (deity) (Na.).
hdryns Hadrian (Na.).
hgy (Hagay) (Na.).
hw he, him/itself (Pa., Ha.); that (demonstrative pronoun) (Na.).
hw' to be, to become (perf. *hwt*, *hww*, impf. *yhw'*, *yh'*, part. *hwn*) (Pa.).
hy she (Na.).
hygmwn governor (ἡγεμών) (Pa.).
hyk b as in, according to (Pa.).
hykl temple (Pa.).
hk' see *mhk'*.
hlydwrs Heliodōros (Pa.).
hlk to die (perf. *hlkt*) (Na. < Ar.).
hn if (Na.). See also *'n*, *lhn*.
hnw them, those (Ha.).

W

w and, (Pa. 20[1]) "who is also" (Pa., Ha., Na.).
w'lt (f.) Wā'ilath (Na.).

whb'lhy Wahballāhī (Na.).
whwb' Wahūbā (read *whyb'?*) (Ha.).
wylt (proper name, reading?) (Ha.).
wld offspring, posterity (Na.).
wqyh'l (Waqīh'el) (Na.).
wrwd Worōd (Pa.).

Z

zbd' Zabdā; *Zbdl'* Zabdilā; *zbdbwl* Zabdibōl; *zby* Zabbay, *bt zby* (f.) Bath Zabbay, Zenobia; *zbyd'* Zebīdā (Pa.).
zbn to buy; *pa.* to sell (Na.).
zbn time (both "temps" and "fois"), *lzbn zbn* at a given time (Pa.).
zdq, f. det. *zdqt'* pious (Pa.).
zyd'l Zayd'el (Na.).
zyd'lt Zayd'allāth (Ha.).
zky victorious, *zky' d gndh ʿm 'lh'* "the victorious one whose Gad (Divine Glory) is with the gods" (epithet of King Sanaṭrūq).
zmn time ("fois") (Na.).
zm' hair = person (suff. *zmth*) (Ha.).
zʿyr small (Na.).
zq (wine) skin (pl. *zqyn*) (Pa.).
zrʿ seed, offspring (Ha.).
zrq' (Zarqā) (Ha.).

Ḥ

ḥbr companion, fellow-member (Na.).
ḥbš see *yḥbš*.
ḥd one (Na.). See also *blḥd*.
ḥdwdn Ḥaddūdān (Pa.).
ḥdy to rejoice (*l* or *b* about) (perf. *ḥdy*, part. *ḥdyn* [reading?]) (Ha.).
ḥdt *pa.* to renew (Na.); *ḥdt* new (Pa.).
ḥwl something unconsecrated (pl. suff. *ḥwlwh*) (Pa.).
ḥwr white, plaster (Pa.).
ḥz' *etp.* to appear appropriate (δεδόχθαι) (perf. *'tḥzy*) (Pa.).
ḥz' (Ḥazā) (Na.).
ḥṭr' Hatra (Ha.).
ḥyyn life (cstr. *ḥyy*, *ḥy'*, *ḥy*, suff. *ḥywhy*, *ḥyyh*, *ḥyyhwn*, *ḥyhn*) (Pa., Ha., Na.).
ḥyb liable (pl. f. *ḥybn*) (Pa.).
ḥyl army, *rb ḥyl' rb'* commander-in-chief (Pa.).
ḥyr' Ḥayrā (Ha.).
ḥyrn Ḥayrān (Pa.).
ḥldw (f.) Ḥuldū (Na.).
ḥlyq' nature, character (cstr. *ḥlyqt*) (Na.).
ḥlpw Ḥalafū (Na.).
ḥlq portion (Na.).
ḥmn altar of incense (Pa., Na.).
ḥmr wine (Pa.); *ḥmr* wine-merchant (Ha.).
ḥmryn (pl.) architectural element in a tomb (columns) (Pa.), cf. Syriac *ḥmurtā*.
ḥmš five, *ḥmš m'h* five hundred (Pa., Na.).
ḥnk to dedicate (Pa.).
ḥsk to save (Pa.).
ḥrg forbidden (object) (Na.).
ḥryš' name of a deity (Ḥarīšā?) (Na.).
ḥrm inviolable (object) (Na.).
ḥrmw (Ḥaramū) (Na.).
**ḥry* liberty, in *br ḥry* freedman of, *bt ḥry* freed-woman of (Pa.).
ḥrt' Ḥertā (f. deity) (Pa.).
ḥrtt Ḥārethath (Ἀρέτας); *ḥrty* (coinage) issued by King Aretas (Na.).
ḥšy except (Na. < Ar.). The *w* that follows in the Na. inscription seems to be a dittography.
ḥšš (Ḥašaš) (Pa.).
ḥtn son-in-law (Na.).

Ṭ

ṭb good, *dkyr lṭb* (Na. *bṭb*) may he be well remembered (Pa., Ha., Na.); *ṭbyt* well (adverb) (Pa.).
ṭbt Ṭebet (= January) (Na.).
ṭwr low wall(?) (Na.).
ṭyṭwylw (proper name) (Pa.).
ṭly temple-page (pl. det. *ṭly'*) (Pa.).
ṭll pa. to cover (with a roof) (Pa.).

Y

**ybš* dry land (det. *ybš'*) (Pa.).
yd hand (Pa., Na.).
yd' *ap̄.* to give thanks, to acknowledge (part. *mwd'*) (Pa.).
ydyʿbl Yedīʿbēl (Pa.).
ydʿ to know (Pa.).
yhb to give (part. pass. *yhyb* given, deposited) (Pa., Na.); *yhb* Yahab (Ha.). See also *mwhbh*.
yhbrmryn Yahabbarmārayn (Ha.).

*ywly*ʾ (f.) Julia; (Pa. 11⁵) (m.) *Iulie* = Julius (Pa.).
ywlys Julius (Pa.).
ywm day (Pa.).
yḥbš (Yaḥboš) (Ha.).
yld *etp.* to be born (impf. *ytyld*); *yld* children (Na.); *yld* birth, in *byld*ʾ (**bt yld*ʾ) house of birth, prob. temple dedicated to the passing of the Divine Glory into the person of the new king (Ha.).
ym sea (Pa.).
ymyn right (hand), south; *ymnyyn*, pl. of (adjective) **ymny* to the right (or mistake for *ymynyn*?) (Pa. 11²) (Pa., Na.).
ysp *ap̄.* to add, to augment (perf. ʾ*wsp*) (Na.).
*y*ʿ*wt* Yaʿūth (Pa.).
yqr honor (Pa.).
yrḥ month (Pa., Ha., Na.).
yrḥbwl Yarḥibōl (deity) (Pa.).
*yrḥbwl*ʾ Yarḥibōlā; *yrḥy* Yarḥay (Pa.).
yt accusative particle (suff. *yth*) (Pa., Na.).
ytb to sit, *ytb* ʿ*l* to preside over (Pa.).
ytyr more, further (Pa.).

K

k (prep.) according to, after the manner of (Na.).
*k*ʾ see *lk*ʾ, *mhk*ʾ.
kd when (Pa.); *kdy* (conj.) when (Pa.), like as (Na.), *kdy b* according to what is contained in . . ., *kdy bhm* whatever they contain (Na.).
khylw Kohaylū (Na.).
khnbw Kāhinnabū (tribal name) (Pa.).
kwh opening (pl. det. *kwt*ʾ) (Na.).
kwl see *kl*.
kwt thus, likewise (Pa.). See also *bdyl*, *mṯl*.
kys money bag, money (Pa.).
kl, (Ha.) *kwl* (rarely *kl*) all, every, entire, everybody, everything (suff. *klh*, *kwlh*, *klhwn*, *kwlhwn*, *klhyn*), also *kl* . . . *klh*; ʾ*nwš* . . . *klh* anybody at all, *ktb klh* any document (Pa., Ha., Na.).
klb dog, *Nrgwl klb*ʾ (the God) Nergal of the dog (Ha.).
*klb*ʾ Kalbā (Na.).
klybt (f.) Kulaybath (Na.).
kmkm (f.) (Kamkam) (Na.).
kmr priest, *kmr*ʾ *rb*ʾ the high priest (Pa., Ha., Na.); *kmr*ʾ priestess (cstr. *kmrt*) (Ha.).
*kmr*ʾ Komarā (tribal name) (Pa.).
knwn Kānūn (= November) (Pa., Ha.).
knwšt (f.) (Kenūshath?) (Na.).
knš to assemble (part. pass. f. *knyš*ʾ) (Pa.).
ksp money (Na.).
*k*ʿ*bw* Kaʿbū (Na.).
kpr tomb (Na.).
*kṣy*ʾ (Kaṣyā) (Ha.).
*kṣry*ʾ Caesars (= *qsry*ʾ, or, less likely, camp [*castra*], soldiers [*qaṣrāyē*] (Ha.).
krk courtyard in front of a tomb (Na.).
ktb to write (perf. pl. *ktb*, impf. *yktb*, [Ha.] *lktwb*, part. pass. *ktyb*; *yktb* [Pa. 6⁸] impf. pass. *p*ʿ*al* or *etp.* with assimilation); *etp.* to be written (part. *mtktb*); *ktb* inscription, writing, document; *ktwb* scribe (Pa., Ha., Na.).
ktl wall (partition).

L

l for, to, to (before inf.), in (his honor), (year . . .) of, (Na. 11⁸) due to, (suff. *lh*, *ln*, *lhm*, *lhn*, *lhwn*) (Pa., Ha., Na.). See also *br*, *gw*, *lqbl*, *mṯl*.
*l*ʾ not (Pa., Ha., Na.).
*lbwš*ʾ see *bwš*ʾ.
lbr, *lgw* see *br*, *gw*.
lgyn legion (pl. det. *lgyny*ʾ) (Pa.).
lhn except (Na.).
lwqys Lucius (Pa.).
lwt *pa.* to make someone (*l*) a partner (Pa.).
lḥytw Luḥītū (place name) (Na.).
*lk*ʾ (in the direction of) here (Pa.).
*l*ʿ*bn* Laʿbān (place name) (Na.).
*l*ʿ*lwh*, *l*ʿ*lyhwn* see ʿ*l*.
*l*ʿ*n* to curse (Na.).
lqbl in front of (Pa.).
lšmš Lišamš (Pa.).

M

mʾh hundred (Pa., Na.).
mdy see *mh.*
mdy Mede(?) (*mdyʾ*, read *mryʾ* "lord"?) (Ha.).
mdynʾ city (cstr. *mdynt*, suff. *mdth*) (Pa.).
mdkʾ in *br mdkʾ* (Ha.), or read *mrkʾ* = *mlkʾ*?
mdnḥ east, *mdnḥ ymynʾ* south east; *mdnḥy* eastern, lying to the east (Pa., Na.).
mdʿm, mndʿm anything, *lmdʿmʾ mdʿmʾ* for each article (Pa., Na.); *mdʿn, bmdʿn* in such a (any) way (manner) (Pa.).
mdth see *mdynʾ.*
mh dy whatever (Na.), *mdy* that which (Pa.).
mhkʾ from here (Ha.).
mhrdd Mihrdād (Pa.).
mhryt promptly (or proper name?) (Pa.).
mhrqr diviner(?) (Pa.).
mwhbh (deed of) gift (Na.).
mwtb throne (?, suff. *mwtbh*) (Na.).
mzbnʾ Mezabbanā (Pa.).
mzg see *mmzgn.*
mḥrmʾ consecrated place (det. *mḥrmtʾ*) (Na.).
mṭy camel-rider (an epithet of Arṣū, cf. *w*) (Pa.).
mṭl kwt therefore, *lmṭl dy* in such a way that (Pa.).
myn water (det. *myʾ*) (Na.).
myt to die (perf. *mytt*) (Ha.).
mytʾ Mītā (tribal name) (Pa.).
mytwytʾ (root *ʾtʾ*) the coming (Pa.).
mks tax, taxation; *mks* tax collector (Pa.).
mlʾ (Malē) (Pa.).
mly (?, Ha. 10^{10}).
mlk king (pl. det. *mlkʾ*) (Pa., Ha., Na.); *mlkʾ* queen (det. *mlktʾ*) (Pa.); *mlkw* kingdom (suff. *mlkwth*) (Ha.); *mlk* Malik (Na.); *mlkw* Mal(i)kū (Pa., Na.); *mlkwsʾ* Malkōsā (Pa.). See also *mdkʾ.*
mmzgn wine-mixer (Pa.).
mn from, belonging to, according to (custom), by (law) (suff. *mnh, mnhm*) (Pa., Ha., Na.). See also *dy, mhkʾ, qdm, tḥt.*
mn, mn dy, (Na. also) *kl mn dy* whoever (Ha., Na.).
mndʿm see *mdʿm.*
mnwʿt (f.) (Menūʿath) (Na.).
mnwtw Manōtū (f. deity) (Na.).
mnt share (suff. *mnth*) (Pa.).
msyʿn helper, assistant (pl. det. *msyʿnʾ*) (Pa.).
mʿynʾ (f.) Muʿaynā (Pa.).
mʿynw Muʿaynū (Na.).
mʿyrw Muʿayrū (Na.).
mʿnʾ Maʿnā (Ha.).
mʿlyk see *ʿll.*
mʿrb west; *mʿrby* western (Pa.).
mʿrʾ cave (det. *mʿrtʾ*) (Pa.).
mprnsn, f. det. *mprnsnytʾ* provider, foster mother (Pa.).
mṣb stele (Pa.).
mqbr tomb (as a whole); *mqbrʾ* (det. *mqbrtʾ*) the same (Na.). See also *qbr.*
mqy Maqqay (Pa.).
mqymw Moqīmū (Pa.).
mqm platter, table top (Ha.).
mrʾ, mr lord, master (suff. *mrʾnʾ*, *mrn* [referring either to a deity or the reigning king], *mrhwn*, pl. suff. *mryn* [in *brmryn*]), *mrʾ ʿlmʾ* Lord of the World, *mry ʿlmʾ* (Na. 15^7 sg.?), *mr bytʾ* lord of the temple (Pa., Ha., Na.); *mrʾ* mistress, Lady (suff. *mrtn* [deity or queen], *mrthwn*) (Pa., Ha.).
mrzḥ religious society, thiasos (Na.); *mrzḥw* (cstr. *mrzḥwt*) the same (Pa.).
mrḥ see *rwḥ.*
mrḥšwn Marḥešwan (= November) (Pa., Ha.).
mrtbw (f.) Martabū (Ha.).
mškb tomb (Na.).
mšknʾ (Maškēnā) (place name) (Ha.).
mšl fork (Pa.).
mšrytʾ (det.) camp (Na.).
mtʾ Mattā (Pa.).
mtqnn (corresponding to Latin) *corrector, restitutor* (Pa.).

N

nʾry Naʾaray (Pa.). Cf. below *nʿry.*
nbwzbd Nabūzabad (Pa.).
nbṭw the Nabataeans (Na.).

nhyr, f. det. *nhyrtʾ* brillant (*illustris*, λαμπρός) (Pa.).
nwyt next to (Pa.).
**nḥrʾ* killing by stabbing, *bt nḥryʾ* (det.) slaughterhouse (Pa.).
nḥš omen (Ha.).
nṭyrʾl Neṭīrʾel (Na.).
nṭr in *bt nṭrʾ* (det. pl.) guard room (Pa.).
nysn Nisan (= April) (Pa., Na.).
nyš emblem, sign (sg. or pl. det. *nyšʾ*) (Ha.).
nkyhwn (Ha. 20^8) perhaps read *nk⟨d⟩yhwn* their descendants.
nmws law (νόμος) (Pa.).
nmr (?, Ha. 10^{11}).
nny Nanay (f. deity) (Pa.).
nsb to take (Pa.).
nsḥt the copy (of a deed) (Na. < Ar.).
nʿry (?) Noʿaray (*Νοαραιου*, perhaps representing *nʾry*) (Pa.).
npq *ap̄*. to take out, to bring forth, to produce (a document) (impf. *ynpq*) (Na.).
npš self (reflexive pronoun, suff *npšh*, *npšhm*), monument (pl. det. *npštʾ*) (Na.).
nṣrw Naṣrū (Ha.).
nrgwl Nergal (deity) (Ha.).
nrqys Narqaios (proper name?) (Pa.).
nšʾ Nešā (Pa., Ha.).
nšwm Naššūm (Pa.).
nšyb kinsman (Na.).
nšrʾ Našrā (deity), or eagle ("our Lord of the eagle") (Ha.).
nšry Našray; *nšryhb* Našaryahab; *nšrʿqb* Našarʿaqab (Ha.).
ntwnʾšryʾ from Natunišar (place name) (Ha.).
ntn to give (away), *ntn w qbr* to give leave to bury (Na.).

S

sgyʾ, *śgyʾ* (pl. m.) *śgyʾyn*, (f.) *śgyn*, *sgyʾn* many (Pa.).
sdqyʾ syndics, public advocates (σύνδικοι) (Pa.).
shd to give testimony; *śhd* witness (Pa.).
sḥrw Saḥrū (deity) (Ha.).
sṭr, *śṭr* side; *sṭr mn* aside from, except (Pa.).
syʿ see *msyʿn*.
slʿ selaʿ (= silver drachma), a monetary unit (Na.).
slyk Seleucus (?) (Ha.).
slq *ap̄*. to bring up, to specify (perf. [pass.?] *ʾsqw*, part. pass. *msq*) (Pa.).
smyʾ, *śmyʾ* Šamayyâ (deity) or Semayā (det.) image, (Ha. 14^2) *rb smyʾ* high priest of S. (?); image, standard (pl. det. *smytʾ*); *bt smy* (f.) Bath (Samay) (Ha.).
smk banquet, *gnt smkʾ* triclinium. (Na.).
sml left (hand); *smly* northern (Pa.).
snṭrq Sanaṭrūq (Ha.).
snqlṭyqʾ senator (συγκλητικός) (Pa.).
sp (det. *spʾ*) praetorium (Pa.).
spṭmyʾ (f.) Septimia; (Pa. 16^2) the *Septimii*.
spṭmyws Septimius (Pa.).
spr writing (Pa.); *spr* scribe (Ha.).
srbn quarrel (Pa.).
stn (Satan) (Ha.).
str *pa*. to protect (Pa.).

ʿ

ʿbd to do, to make (perf. pl. *ʿbdw*, *ʿbd*, perf. suff. *ʿbdh*, impf. *yʿbd*); *pᵊʿīl* to be executed (perf. *ʿbydt*); *etp*. to be done (impf. *ytʿbd*) (Pa., Ha., Na.). See also *ʿbydʾ*.—Proper names composed with *ʿbd*: *ʿbdʾlgʾ* ʿAbdʾalgā (Na.); *ʿbdʾly* ʿAbdʾilay (Ha.); *ʿbdbl* ʿAbdibēl (Pa.); *ʿbdl* see *bwšʾ*; *ʿbdmlyk* ʿAbdmalīk (ʿAbdmulayk?) (Ha.); *ʿbdmnwtw* ʿAbdmanōtū (Na.); *ʿbdsmyʾ* ʿAbdsemayyā (ʿAbdsemaya?) (Ha.); *ʿbdʿbdt* ʿAbdʿobodath (Na.); *ʿbdʿstwr* ʿAbdʿastōr (Pa.); *ʿbdšbl* (reading?) (Ha.); *ʿbdšlmʾ* ʿAbdšalmā (Ha.).
ʿbdt ʿObodath (deity) (Na.).
ʿbydʾ work (det. *ʿbydtʾ*), (cstr.) *ʿbydt* in the form of (Na. 4^1), pl. *ʿbydn* goods (Pa., Na.).
ʿbydw ʿObaydū (Na.).
ʿbsʾ ʿAbissā (Ha.).
ʿbr to pass (*b* by) (impf. *lʿbwr*) (Ha.).
ʿbrtʾ ʿAbarta (place name) (Na.).
ʿgʾ ʿOgā (Pa.).
ʿgylw ʿOgeilū (Pa.); *ʿgyly* ʿOgeilay (Ha.).

ʿglbwl ʿAglibōl (deity) (Pa.).
ʿd until, (in addition) to (Na.).
ʿdʾ (f.) ʿAddā (Pa.).
ʿdr to support (Pa.).
ʿwdw ʿAwdū (Ha.).
ʿzyzw ʿAzīzū (Pa.).
ʿyd custom (Pa.).
ʿydw ʿAydū (Na.).
ʿyn spring (source) (Pa., Na.).
ʿyq see *ʿqʾ*.
ʿyr *pa.* to change (Na. < Ar.); *ʿyr* other, someone else except, *kʿyr dnh* otherwise, suff. *ʿyrh* other than it, anything else (Na.).
ʿl on, over, against, for (in favor of), concerning, during (the years), (suff. *ʿlwhy*, *ʿlyh*, *ʿlyhwn*), *hwʾ ʿl* to be in charge cf (Pa., Ha., Na.); *lʿlwh ʿl*, *lʿlyhwn* (introduces the object of "to widen," Pa. $9^{9,11}$).
ʿlʾ above (adverb), *ʿlʾ mn* above (prep.), *ʿly* (< Ar.) *mn* above (prep.) (Na.).
ʿlyy ʿOlayyay (Pa.).
ʿlym young man, servant (Na.).
ʿll to enter (impf. *lʿwl*) (Ha.), *mʿlyk* (inf. suff.) when you enter (Pa.).
ʿlm world, eternity (Pa., Na.). See also *mrʾ*.
ʿltʾ (det.) altar (Pa.).
ʿm (together) with (suff. *ʿmh*) (Pa., Ha., Na.), *ʿm ʾlhʾ* (his *gnd* is) with the gods (= is deceased).
ʿm people (suff. *ʿmh*) (Na.).
ʿmʾlhʾ ʿAmʾelāhā (Ha.).
ʿmwd column (pl. det. *ʿmwdʾ*, reading uncertain, possibly *ʿqwrʾ* meaning unkown) (Pa.).
ʿmnd (ʿAmnad) (place name) (Na.).
ʿmr life, career (Pa.).
ʿnh to answer (one's prayer) (suff. *ʿnn*) (Pa.).
ʿnmw ʿAnimū (Na.).
ʿqʾ distress (Pa.).
ʿqbʾ in *bt ʿqbʾ* (place name) (Ha.).
ʿqbr read *ʿqrb*.
ʿqwbšmš ʿAqūbšamaš (Ha.).
ʿqwr see *ʿmwd*.
ʿqrb ʿAqrab (Na.).
ʿrb the Arabs; *ʿrbwʾw* region in northern Mesopotamia around Hatra (Ha.).
ʿrkwtʾ (pl. det.) portico (Na.).
ʿśryn twenty; *ʿśrtʾ* the Ten (an administrative unit, *δεκάπρωτοι*) (Pa.).
ʿtyq old (Pa.).

P

p and, in this case, introduces apodosis after conditional clause (whoever, if someone . . .) (Na.).
pzgrybʾ, *pšgry⟨b⟩ʾ* heir apparent (Ha. < Parthian).
pḥd clan, tribe (Pa.).
pḥm (Paḥam) (Na.).
py in (Na. < Ar.).
plg to be in the middle of (perf. pl. *plg*, Pa. 11^9); *plg* half; *plgw* half (cstr. *plgwt*) (Pa.).
plhdrwtʾ (det.) presidency, office of the *πρόεδρος* (Pa.).
plḥ worshiper (Ha.).
plpṭr Philopatōr (Pa.).
psl mason, sculptor (Na.).
pṣṣ *etpa.* to be removed (impf. *ytpṣṣ*) (Na.).
pqdwn order, responsibility (Na.).
prṭnks Pertinax (Pa.).
prmwn Phirmōn, in (f.) *bt prmwn.*
prns see *mprnsn.*
prsqs Priscus (Pa.).
pšgryʾ see *pzgrybʾ*.
ptwrʾ diviner(?) (Na.).
ptḥ to open (impf. suff. *yptḥh*) (Na.).
ptr table (for ritual use) (Ha.).

Ṣ

ṣbʾ to want, to be willing (*dy* plus impf.: to do something); *ṣbw* matter, case (pl. det. *ṣbwtʾ*) (Pa.).
ṣhwtʾ (pl. det.) façade (Na.).
ṣlm statue, likeness, *ṣlmʾ* (cstr. *ṣlmt*, det. *ṣlmtʾ*), if the representation is that of a woman (Pa., Ha.).
ṣnʿ to make (perf. suff. *ṣnʿh*) (Na. < Ar.).
ṣryḥ funerary chamber (Na.).

Q

qbl *pa.* to face (part. *mqblyn*) (Pa.). See also *lqbl*.
qbr to bury (impf. *yqbr*, inf. *mqbr*); *etp.* to be buried (impf. *ytqbr*,

ytqbrwn); *qbr*, (Ar.) *ʾlqbrw* tomb (Na.). See also *mqbr*.

qdm, *mn qdm* (*qm*) before (prep., local) (suff. *qmwhy* [mistake for *qdmwhy*?], *qdmyhm*) (Ha., Na.); *qdmy* former (det. *qdmyʾ*, pl. det. *qdmyʾ*) (Pa.).

qdš *pa.* to sanctify (part. pass. *mqdšyn*); *qdš* sanctuary, shrine (pl. suff. *qdšwhy*) (Pa.).

qwm to stand, to be located (part. f. *qymʾ*; part. [or adj. *qayyâm*?] *qym* "legitimate, valid," with *ʿl* "in charge of"); *ap̄.* to set up, to erect (perf. *ʾqym* [*ʾyqym*], *ʾqymt* [*ʾyqymt*], pl. *ʾqymw* [*ʾyqmw*], *ʾqym*) (Pa., Ha., Na.).

qṭyr in *bqṭyrʾ* by force (Ha.).

qṭl to kill (perf. suff. *qṭlh*) (Ha.)

qym see *qwm*.

qymy (f.) (Qayyāmay) (Ha.).

qysr (Na.), *qsr* (Pa.) Caesar (*καῖσαρ*). See also *kṣryʾ*.

qyšh Qayšā (deity), *byt qyšʾ* temple of—(Na.).

qldys Claudius (Na.).

qlnyʾ colony (*colonia*) (Pa.).

qm see *qdm*.

qnh creator, possessor (Ha.).

qns fine, money payment (Na.).

qsm divination (Pa.).

qsntn Qosnatan (Na.).

qsr see *qysr*.

qṣyw Qaṣyū (Na.).

qrʾ to call, to invoke (perf. *qrlh* [< *qrʾ lh*], *qrw*, suff. *qrh*, impf. suff. [Ha.] *lqryhy*, imp.[?] *qry*, inf. *lqrt* [?, Hatra 17⁵ "in order to invoke the gods"]; *etp.* to be called, named (part. *mtqrʾ*) (Pa., Ha., Na.).

qrb *pa.* to offer (a gift to a deity) (Pa.).

qrṭsṭʾ, *qrṭsṭwʾ* (pl. det.) excellent (*κρά-τιστοι*) (Pa.).

qryʾ village (det. *qrytʾ*) (Pa.).

qrspynws Crispinus (Pa.).

qšt archer (pl. det. *qštʾ*) (Pa.).

R

rʾš head, chief (Na.).

rb great, large, (noun) chief, *kmrʾ rbʾ* high priest (see also *smyʾ*), *rb ʿyn* lord of spring (Efca), *rb ʾsyrʾ* Lord of the Fettered (name of a deity?, *Ραβασειρη*). See also *ḥyl*.

rbʾl Rabbʾel (Pa.).

rbwʿʾ recess (det. *rbwʿtʾ*) (Pa.).

rbytʾ steward (Ha.).

rbnw office of president (cstr. *rbnwt*) (Pa.).

rhn to give in pledge, to mortgage (Na.).

rwḥ space; *rwḥʾ* widening, ease (of spirit) (opp. *ʿqʾ*) (Pa.).

rwḥ in *mrḥ* (= *mn rḥ*) side, direction (Na.).

rwmʾ Rawmā (Na.).

rzʾyn (pl.) expenses (Pa.).

rḥḥ (?) to widen (impf. *yrḥ*, inf. *mrḥ*) (Pa.).

rḥm to love (imp. suff. *rḥmh*, part. *rḥm*) (Ha., Na.); *rḥym* loving (Pa., Ha.); *rḥmnʾ* the Merciful, Compassionate (deity) (Pa.).

rḥq to cede (perf. *rḥqt*, pl. f. *rḥq*) (Pa.).

rybmt (f.) (Rībamat??) (Na.).

rʿ earth (det. *rʿʾ* < *ʾrʿʾ*) (Ha.).

rqwš (f.) (Rāqōš?) (Na.).

ršy permitted (Na.).

ršp Reshef (deity) (Pa.).

Ś

śgyʾ see *sgyʾ*.

śhd see *shd*.

śḥq to laugh (impf. suff. *lśḥqh* "smiles at him kindly") (Ha.).

śṭr see *sṭr*.

śmyʾ see *smyʾ*.

Š

šʾl *ap̄.* to lend (perf. *ʾšʾlt*) (Pa.).

šʾry rest, remainder (cstr. *šʾryt*) (Na.).

šbz (read *šbw*?, Parthian proper name) (Ha.).

šbʿ seven (Pa., Na.).

šhymw Šohaymū (Pa.).

šwq market, *rb šwq ἀγορανόμος* (Pa.).

šḥym secular, not consecrated (f. det. *šḥymtʾ*) (Pa.).

šḥrw Šaḥrū (deity) (Ha.).

šṭr document, deed, *bšṭry ḥrmyn* according to the documents concerning inviolable objects (Pa., Na.).

šyd plasterer (Na.).

škybl Šokaybēl (Pa.).
škytyt honorably (Pa.).
škn see *mškn*.
šlw limb (of body) (Na.).
šlṭ to command; *šlṭwn* authority, jurisdiction, see *byt* (Na.); *šlyṭ l* authorized, having the right to (Pa.).
šlm peace, well-being (Na.); *šlmw* the Šalamians (people) (Na.); *šlmn* Šalmān (Pa.); *šlymt* (f.) Šalīmath (Pa., Na.); *šlmt* (f.) Šalmath (Pa.).
šm name (suff. *šmh*) (Pa.).
šmʿ to hear (Pa.).
šmd curse (pl. *šmdyn*) (Na.).
šmš *pa.* to serve, to worship (Pa.).
šmš Šamaš (deity) (Ha.).
šmšbrk Šamašbarak (Ha.).
šmšlṭb Šamašleṭāb (Ha.).
šnʾ *pa.* to alter (impf. *yšnʾ*); *etpa.* to be altered (impf. *ytšnʾ*) (Na.).
šnh year (cstr. *šnt*, det. *štʾ*, pl. *šnyn*, *šny*), *ʿl šny* during the time of . . . (Pa., Ha., Na.). See also *br*.
šnpyr see *špr*.
šʿʾ (Saʿā?) (Pa.).
šʿdʾ see *oršʿdʾ*.
šʿydw Šaʿīdū (Na.).
špr to please (Pa.); *šnpyr* good (Ha.).
šrr *ap̄.* to establish, to decree (perf. *ʾšr* [sg. with the subject understood, or pl.?], *ʾšrt*) (Pa.).
štʾ see *šnʾ*.
štʾ six (Pa., Na.); *štyn* sixty (Na.); *šttʾ* (det.) the sixth (Pa.).

T

tgr merchant (pl. det. *tgryʾ*, *tgrʾ*) (Pa.).
tdmwr Tadmōr, Palmyra (Pa.).
th this (f.) (Na. < Ar.).
twn chamber, bedroom (Pa.).
tḥt in *mn ltḥt* below (Pa.).
tybwl Taybbōl (Pa.).
tymw Taymū (Na.).
tyr merciful (Pa.).
tkdm (*bt tkdm*: proper name of uncertain reading) (Ha.).
tltʾ three (Pa.); *tltyn* thirty (Na.); *tlt* one third, *tltyn tryn* two thirds (Na.).
tmwz Tammūz (= July) (Na.).
tmnyʾ eight (Pa.).
tnʾ contract (Na.).
tnn here (Pa.).
tqn see *mtqnn*.
tqp strong, valid, *ktb tqp* warrant (Na.).
trn (Pa.), *tryn* (Na.), f. cstr. *trty* (Na.) two.
trʿ gate, door (Pa., Na.).
tšʿ nine (Na.).
tšry Tishri (= October) (Pa., Na., Ha.).

V. JEWISH PALESTINIAN ARAMAIC

(Eduard Yechezkel Kutscher)

(◇ indicates words and word formations that have remained unknown to the existing dictionaries, or words with meanings not listed in them.

° indicates that the vocalization of a word so marked is attested as Palestinian.

The vocalization presents a difficult problem, and the following procedure has been adopted in this glossary:

The vocalization of the Onkelos-type Targum has been used as a basis, because it is most fully known. For it, and only for it, the dictionary of G. H. Dalman (*Aramäisch-Neuhebräisches Handwörterbuch*, 2nd ed. [Frankfurt 1922], IVf.) can be used with profit. However, this vocalization very often does not conform to what was, or can be assumed to have been, true Palestinian (Galilean) usage.

A vocalization of Palestinian origin has become known to some extent through the Targum texts published by P. Kahle (*Masoreten des Westens*, II [Stuttgart 1930]). This vocalization, however, is vulgar in character and, therefore, must be used with caution at the present stage of our knowledge. *Qameṣ* and *pataḥ* have been changed where necessary to conform to normative vocalization. This involves no danger of error, since the true value of the respective vowel signs is easily identifiable by their behavior, *qameṣ* never being reduced to *šewa*. A similar situation exists in the case of the *šewa* and *ḥaṭep̄* vowels, which may be expressed by a full vowel or, like the other vowels, be omitted altogether. The restoration of the often missing *dageš* also seems to involve no risk, and the standard vocalization has, therefore, been employed in this respect, except in a few cases of *dageš lene*, especially after *r* (for instance, מרתוק). In other cases, the "vulgar" vocalization has been retained. This is no doubt fully justified in the case of *segol*, since it appears to be a free variant of both *pataḥ* and *ṣere* (cf. כְּסַף, כְּסֵף, כְּסֶף, and the problematic fourth form כֶּסֶף). Sometimes, it has not been easy to reach a decision concerning the use of *qameṣ*, for instance, רָמשה (cf. the spelling רמוש in Galilean texts). No consistency in all these respects is at yet possible, and often the safest procedure seems to be to accept whatever is attested. Occasionally, transliterations, both Greek (cf. פורדס) and Latin (cf. תורדין), may be decisive. In other cases, it was considered preferable to omit any attempt at vocalization.

At times, the vocalization of Biblical Aramaic has been included, as in אלף. In some cases, the Syriac vocalization has been adopted (e. g., אכסני), in others that of Mishnaic Hebrew (Mishna Ms. Kaufmann) (e. g. טיבור).

Where the vocalization of the abs. state is not attested, the form, if any, for which it is known has been noted.

Nearly all final long *ās*, both in the feminine ending and in the det. sg., are spelled with ה in conformity with general Palestinian usage.

Occurrences of verbal forms in the *eṯp.*, *eṯpa.*, and *ettap̄.* have as a rule not been listed, whenever their meaning is merely the passive or reflexive of a listed *pᵊʿal*, *pa.*, or *ap̄.*)

א

א׳ abbreviation of אמר, אמרין, etc.

אַב father, pl. אֲבָהָן; אַבָּא, °אֶבָּא° my (our) father.

אבא (proper name).

אבד to perish; *ap̄.* to destroy. See also יבידה.

אבהוא (proper name).

אבון (proper name).

אֶבֶן, °אֲבֵן°, °אֲבֶן° (f.) stone.

אבר׳, אַבְרָם, אַבְרָהָם Abraham.

אגו מן let us go! (Greek ἄγωμεν, ἄγε μήν?) (cf. Theodor-Albeck, 925).

אגר to hire, to employ; °אֲגִיר° hired man; °אֲגַר° wages, pay, (doctor's) bill, reward, compensation.

אִיגָּר roof (Akk.).

אִיגְּרָה letter (Akk.).

אֱדַיִן, בֶּאדַיִן then.

°אֲדַם° blood.

אדמדמני overripe grapes (cf. I. Löw, *Die Flora der Juden*, I, 81).

אָדוֹן (H.) lord.

אדן (f.) ear, det. אֶדְנָה.

°אוֹ° or, אוֹ ... אוֹ either ... or.

אֲוֵיר air (Greek ἀήρ).

°אוליסיס° glassworks (Greek *ὑάλωσις?, cf. S. Lieberman, in *Tarbiz*, III [1932], 208 n. 7).

אוּרַיָּה (ותומיה) Urim (and Thummim).

אוֹרָיָה Torah, det. אוֹרָיְתָה.

אזה to heat.

אזל to go, to go away.

°אַח° brother; °אֲחָת° sister.

אַחְסָנָה property.

(אחר) after (prep.); לְאַחֲרָא, אחר, backwards; אָחֳרָן, אָוחֳרָן, °אוֹחַרַן°, °אַחֲרַן° (!), חורן other, pl. f. אָחֳרָנְיָין.

אייבו (proper name).

°אִידִ°, °אֶידִ° see יד.

°אֵידָא° (f.) which, אידא ד־ that which (f.). See also הידה.

אֵימָה fear.

°אִימָם° see ימם.

°אִיקָר° see יקר.

°אִית° there is, there exists, אִית ד־ some, אית...אית whether ...or.

אכל to eat, (H.) impf. יֹוכַל.

אַכְסְנָי stranger (Greek ξένος).

אכף to concern, מה אכף לך what do you care?

אֵל God.

אִילָּא, אֶלָּא (אֵילָא, אֵלָא), °אִלָּא° (!) but, except, אלא ... לא only (without *dageš* in Yemenite tradition).

אלד see אלה.

°אֱלָהּ° god; אלד (for אלה) God.

אִילּוּ if; °אִילּוּ מני ד־° if ... not (cf. Theodor-Albeck, 335f.); °אִילּוּלֵי° if ... not.

אֵלוֹנֵי מַמְרֵה Terebinths of Mamre.

אלכסנדרון Alexander the Great.

אִילֵּן°, אִילֵּיֵין°, אֵלֵּין° these, those, אִילֵּן ד־ those belonging to, the adherents of.

אֱלִיעֶזֶר (אֶלְעָזָר) Eliezer (Eleazar).

אלף, ילף to learn; *pa.* to teach; אוּלְפָּן instruction.

אֲלַף, אֶלֶף thousand.

אֵם, אֵים mother.

אמ׳ abbreviation of אֲמַר, אֲמְרָה, etc.

אַמָּה cubit, pl. אַמִּין.

אַמְהָה° maid servant.

אִימָם° see ימם.

אָמֵן amen (H.).

אמן see הימן.

אוּמָּנוּ trade, occupation.

אמר to say, to speak, to tell, to command, דמר = דאמר.

אִימַּר lamb.

אָן° where?, אן ד־ where, cf. also הן; מנן (< מן אן) from where?

אֶן°, אֶין° if.

אֵן°, אֶן°, אֶין° yes. See also הן.

אֲנָה°, אֲנָא° I.

אנגריה forced labor, דנגריה = דאנגריה (Greek ἀγγαρεία).

אנטיגרפה reply to a letter (Greek ἀντιγραφή).

אנטוכייה Antioch.

אנטונינוס Antoninus (Roman Emperor).

אנטיפוטה proconsul (Greek ἀνθύπατος).

אֲנַן°, אֲנַן we.

אֱנוּן°, אִנּוּן°, אִינּוּן they, them, those (m.). See also הנון.

אוֹנֶס force, compulsion.

אֲנָשׁ°, אֱנוֹשׁ man, people.

אִנְתָּה see אתה.

אִיסְטְלֵי° (אֶסטֹליתה°) robe (Greek στολή).

אסי *pa.* to heal (Ex. 29:19 *pəʿal*); אָסֵי° physician.

אסי proper name.

איסכולסטיקה scholar (Greek σχολαστικός).

אֲסַן bush, det. אֲסַנָּה.

(אַף) pl. אַפִּין° face, modes, ways (suff. אַפֵּיךְ°); עַל אַפֵּי (prep.) opposite. See also נסב.

אַף, אוּף also, further.

אֲפִילוּ even, אפילו ד־ even if.

אפס proper name.

אפסד° loss, suff. אַפְסְדֵהּ°.

אֶפְרַיִם Ephraim.

איפרכיה province (Greek ἐπαρχία).

אפתי רמש toward evening.

אוֹצַר storehouse.

אִיקָר see יְקָר.

אַרְבַּע° four; אַרְבַּע עֶשְׂרֵי° fourteen.

אַרְגְּוָן purple.

ארגינט, ארגינטי a demon.

אֹרַח way, det. אָרְחָה°.

אֲרֵי because (conj.).

אַרְיֵה lion, det. אַרְיָיה, אַרְיָה, pl. אַרְיָוָן.

ארך length, det. אֻרְכָּה; אֲרִיךְ long.

אַרְכוֹן, ארכונטס city magistrate, prefect (Greek ἄρχων, gen. ἄρχοντος).

אֲרוּם°, אֲרוֹם° because (conj.). (Pal. Targum Gen. 31:42, etc., for H. כי).

אַרְמְלָה° widow.

ארס *pa.* to betrothe.

ארסקינס Ursicinus (proper name).

אֲרַע (f.), earth, land, country, det. אַרְעָה°.

אֶשׁ° (f.) fire; אִישָּׁה fire, det. אִישָּׁתָה, אֶשְׁתָּה°, אֶישָּׁתָה°.

אֶשְׁכֹּל Eshcol.

אָשֵׁר Asher.

אישתי see שתי.

אַתְּ° (m. and f.) you (sg.).

אתה to come, אתון לכון go!; *aṗ.* to bring; *hoṗ.* to be brought.

אֶתָּה°, אִיתָּה, אֶיתָּה°, אֵיתָּה°, אֶנְתָּה°, woman, wife, pl. נְשִׁין°.

אַתּוּן (m., also f. ?) you (pl.).

אֲתַר place.

אֶתְרֹג a citrus fruit, pl. אֶתְרֹגִּין (אֶתְרֹגִין) (for גּ, cf. the Mishna Ms. Kaufmann, as well as Syriac and Arabic).

ב

ב in, within, with, through, for (price).

באש *aṗ.* to do harm.

בַּבְלָי Babylonian.

בדר *pa.* to scatter.

בהֵית to be ashamed.

בוטה (proper name).

בזז to rob, to plunder; בִּזָּה plunder, spoils.

בֶּזְיוֹן° disgrace, דב׳ shameless.

בחר to choose, to select.

בֶּטְלוֹן⋄ idleness, loss of time.

בי, ביי⋄, ב⋄ house, cstr. בֵּית, suff. בַּיְתָךְ°, pl. בָּתִּין; בכנִישְׁתה synagogue; בֵּית דִּין court (of law); בֵּית לָחֶם Bethlehem; בית מותב dwelling place; בֵּית מַקְדְּשָׁה temple; בֵּית מִשְׁכַּב bed; בֵּית שָׁפַּר° the best of.

בן⋄, בֵּין°, בֵּינֵי° between; בֵּין ... וּבֵין between ... and, either ... or.

ביר׳ = בירבי (< בר רבי) son of a rabbi (Rabbi ....).

בִּירָה fortress, castle.

בִּישׁ (< בְּאִישׁ) bad, evil, wrong.

בכה to weep; בכי weeping.

בְּכֵין, בְּכֵן then.

בכר first-born, det. בּוּכְרָה, בְּכוֹרָה°; בְּכֵירוּ status of first-born; בַּכִּירִ° early, from ancient times.

בִּכְרִי (proper name).

בלדר courier (Latin *veredarius*).

בולווטס councilman (Greek βουλευτής).

בֵּן = בֵּין.

בנה to build.

בני bath (Greek βαλανεῖον).

בִּנְיָמִן Benjamin.

בְּנִין see בַּר.

בְּנָן see בר(ה).

בּוּסֶם perfume, spices.

בסר *pa.* to despise.

בעה *pᵊʿal*, *etp.* to want, to desire, to seek.

בעין (proper name).

בְּעֵל, בְּעֵיל master, husband; בְּעֵל דְּבָב enemy. See also פלגו.

°בְּעִיר cattle, det. °בְּעֶירָה, °בְּעִירָה; בְּעִיר דַּקִּיק small cattle.

בּוּצִין candle, lamp.

בצר to take away.

בַּקְעָה, °בִּקְעָה valley.

בקר *pa.* to permit cattle to graze in.

°בַּר son, pl. °בְּנִין; °בַּרְנָשׁ, בַּר אֱנָשׁ (אנוש) person, pl. בְּנֵי נָשׁ; בַּר בְּרֵהּ ד– the grandson of . . . ; בַּר דְּכַר male offspring; (שִׁמְעוֹן) בַּר כשבה Simeon Bar Kochba (leader of the Jewish revolt against the Romans); בר עולה proper name; בְּרָה daughter, pl. °בְּנָן (sg. suff. °בְּרְתֵּיהּ is Western Aram., cf. Maʿlūla *berčaḥ*, whereas Onkelos בְּרַתֵּיהּ corresponds to the form found in Eastern Aram. dialects, cf., for instance, T. Nöldeke, in *Zeitschrift der Deutschen Morgenländischen Gesellschaft*, XXXVII [1883], 599). See also ח(ו)ר(י)ן.

°בַּר field, °חֵיוַת בָּרָה wild animal.

בָּרֵי, בָּרֵה Creator.

בַּרְזֶל iron (H.).

ברך *pa.* to bless; בְּרִיךְ blessed; בִּרְכָה, det. °בֶּרְכַּתָה (!) blessing.

בְּרַם but.

°בְּתוּלָה virgin.

°בָּתַר (< באתר) after (prep.).

ג

גַּב from, by, to, with; לְגַב, גַּבֵּי at, with, לְגַבֵּי to, by.

גב see גו.

גבל to squeeze.

גבל (place name).

°גְּבַר man, det. °גַּבְרָה, °גּוּבְרָה, pl. גַּבְרִין, °גּוּבְרִין, °גּוֹבְרִין; גִּיבָּר hero, strong man; גְּבָרוּ mighty deed; גְּבוּרָה valor, might, mighty deed.

גָּד Gad.

°גְּדִישׁ heap of sheaves.

°גוֹ, בְּגוֹ amidst, in; מִן גוֹ (גּוֹא) ד– since (conj.); בְּגַוֵּהּ, °בְּגַבַּהּ (to be read בְּגַוַּהּ) because of ... (cf. G. Dalman, Grammatik, 2nd ed., 104f.).

וגו' (H.) and so on.

גוח *ap̄.* to wage (קרב war).

גזה to repay, to punish.

גזר to order, to decree, to circumcise.

גחך to laugh, to jest (מגחך = מן גחך).

גיבת שמו (place name).

גִ(י)חון Gihon.

גין, -ד °בְּגֵין, °בְּגִין because, since (conj.), בגין כדין therefore.

גלג *pa.* to reveal, to boast.

גלה to go into exile, to be exiled, to reveal.

גוליי̈ר a kind of soldier's servant (Latin *galearius*).

גִּלְעָד Gilead.

גמל (חסד) to do good, to be kind.

גַּמְלִיאֵל Gamaliel.

גְּמִיר holocaust, whole offering.

גנב to steal; °גַּנָּב thief; °גְּנֵבָה, °גְּנֵבָה theft.

גנן *ap̄.* to defend, to protect (על someone).

גְּנֵיסַר Gennesaret.

גונתי Goth, servant.

געה to bellow.

גּוֹפֶן vine.

גַּר young animal.

גרזמי fruit, dessert (Greek *γάρισμα).

גרם bone, (det. גַּרְמָה), reflexive pronoun (גַּרְמַהּ herself, מִן גַּרְמוֹן on their own).

גַּרְמִי (proper name).

ד

°ד, °דִּי relative pronoun, he who, that which, genitive particle, introducing direct speech, introducing subordinate clauses (that, so that, because), דבית those of. See also -דיד, -דיל, היא, כד, כדי.

°דָּא, דָּה this (f.).

דְּבָב see בעל דבב.

דבק to reach.

דבר to lead, to seize, to take.

°דְּהַב gold.

דָּוִד David.

דון to pass sentence.

דון see כדון.

דחף to push.

דִּי see ד.

°-דִּיד, -דִּיל independent possessive pronoun; בדילהא for her sake.

°דִּין law, punishment; °דַּיָּן judge.

דֵּין see דֵּן.

דִּיקִי justice, just case (Greek δίκη).

דָּיַר inhabitant.

דכה to be clean, innocent.

דוכס, דוקס commander (Latin *dux*).

דכר to remember, דְּכִיר remembered; דִּכְרָן memory.

°דְּכוּר, דכר male.

דְּכַר ram, pl. °דֶּכְרִין, °דִּכְרִין.

°דַּלְמָא, ד– °דַּלְמָא perhaps.

°דליק טיינא derisive(?) transformation of the name of the Roman Emperor Diocletian.

דְּמוּ image, vision.

דמך to sleep, to die.

דמר see אמר.

°דֵּן, °דֵּין, °דֶּין, °דְּנָא, דְּנָה this (m.); כדן thus, מהו כדן what is the matter?

דָּן Dan.

דנח to rise (sun), to shine.

דֵּינָר denarius (Greek δηνάριον).

דִּיסְקוֹס disk, plate (Greek δίσκος).

דיסקירין, דייסקרה plate (Greek δισκάριον).

°דִּיפְּלָה double (Greek διπλά).

דוקלטינוס, דוקלטיינוס Diocletian.

דַּקִּיק small.

דְּרַג step (of a staircase), det. דַּרְגָּה.

דרך to tread, to walk.

דָּרוֹם south; דָּרוֹמָי southern; דָּרוֹמָה a region of Palestine.

דַּרְמֶשֶׂק Damascus.

דְּרָע arm.

דרש to teach, to lecture, to expound.

ה

°הָא behold, here is.

הָא כְ– see היך.

°הָאֶלַּיִין these.

°הָדָא, °הָדָה this (f.).

הדה see הידה.

°הָדֵן, °הָדֵין, °האדן this (m.).

הֲדַס myrtle branch, pl. הֲדַסִּין.

הַהוּא, f. הַהִיא that (demonstrative pronoun); הַהִיא אִתְּתָא referring to the speaker herself ("I") or to the woman addressed ("you").

הוֹ וַי woe! See also ווי.

הוּא he; מהוא = מה הוא.

(הוד) °לְהוֹד only, but. See also חד.

הוה, הווה to be (perf. הֲוָתֵיהּ = הות ליה, impf. יהא, יהי, תהי, °תאה, °תי; part. הָוֵה consequently; part. pass. (+ אנא) הֲוֵינָא I was).

הוך to go.

°הִיא, הִי she; דהיא (...) כל see כל.

°הַיְדָה, הֵדָה, הַיְדָה which one (f.).

היידיליה behold here he is.

הַיְדֵן which one (m.).

°הֵיךְ, °הֶיךְ, הָא כְ– how?, like, as, הֵיךְ מָה° ד– like that which.

הֵיכַל temple.

הימן part. pass. °מְהַיְמַן, מְהֵימַן reliable; מימנתי (m. and f., also pl.) = מהימנ(ה) יתי believe me.

הָכָא, הָכָה here.

°הַלָא° (= הֲלָא ?) introducing a negative question = strong assertion.

°הילייה° shouts of joy (during a wedding).

הלך *pa.* to walk.

הֶין yes. See also אן.

°הָן° see אן; הָן ד- there where; לְהָן whither, מִן הָן from where.

הנה to please; *eṯpa.* to make use (ב- of); *ap̄.* to profit; הַנִי ל- (for the vocalization, cf. Syriac) pleasing to.

הִנּוּן, הִינּוּן, אִנּוּן, f. הִינִּין they.

הפך to turn, הפך קדל to turn around.

התם there (a loan from Eastern Aram. ? Scribal error ?).

ו

ו and.

וַיי woe! See also הו ויי.

°וְלַד° child, offspring, embryo, suff. °וַלְדַהּ°.

(ות) °כְּוָת° like; דכוות like as; °לְוָת° to, with (French "chez"), מִלְוָת from.

ז

זְבוּלוּן Zebulun.

זבידה (proper name).

זבן to buy; *pa.* to sell; °זְבִינוּ° purchase; זְבִינִין objects of a purchase.

זג garment (Greek ζυγόν ?).

זֵיהוֹר brightness, splendor; זְהוֹרִי crimson.

°זאוויי°, זָוִי corner, place.

זון to nourish, to support.

°זִיו° glory, splendor.

זין *pa.* to arm.

זכה *eṯp.* to be innocent, free; *pa.* to give alms; זָכוּ (religious) merit, meritorious deed.

זמה to fine (< Greek ζημία).

°זְמַן° time, det. °זְמְנָה°, pl. זִמְנִין, °זְמְנִין°, (°תִּנְיָינוּת°) זְמַן תִּנְיָין a second time, זמנין sometimes.

זמר to sing.

זעזע to shake, to disturb.

זעף to reprimand. (ב- someone).

°זעור° small (cf. *Tarbiz*, XXII [1950–51], 53 [offprint, 17]).

זיק skin (for water, wine), pl. זִיקִין.

זיקוק spark.

זקף to put (someone) back (on his feet).

זַרע seed, offspring.

ח

חבב *pa.* to love.

חבל *ap̄.* to injure.

חֲבַר, f. חַבְרָה friend, fellow being, other, Fellow (as a scholarly title).

חֶבְרוֹן Hebron.

°חֶבְרִי (f.) wound.

חבש to imprison.

°חבשובה, חדבשובה Sunday (cf. *Tarbiz*, XXI [1949–50], 205 [offprint, 16]).

°חַד, f. °חֲדָא one; כַּחֲדָא together; °לַחֲדָא very; (חוד) לְחוֹד but; לְחוֹדוֹי, °לְבַלְחוֹדוֹי, לבלחדוי by himself, alone.

חדה to be glad, to rejoice.

חדבשובה see חבשובה.

חוב to sin (מן against), to be found guilty; *pa.* to find guilty.

חוי *pa.* to reveal, to inform.

חִיוְיִ, °חִוְיָ serpent.

חור *pa.* (= *pᵊʿal*) to be white, to shine.

חורן Ḥaurān (region),

חזה to see, חָזֵה ל- (rather חֲזֵה ל-, cf. Mishnaic H. ראוי ל-) fitting; *ettap̄.* to appear.

חַזָּן, חַזָּאן sexton.

חזק *etp.* to exert oneself.

חִזְקִיָּה Hezekiah.

חזר to return, to draw back, to go backwards, חזר בה he changed his mind, חזרת וחמת she saw again; *pᵊʿal*, *pa.* to give back; *ap̄.* to turn (trans.). See also מחזרו.

חֲזִיר swine.

חיוה see בר.

°חִיטָּה wheat, pl. חִיטִּין.

°חֲטָי sin.

חטף to seize, to snatch.

חוטר staff, det. °חוּטְרָה.

חיה to live; חי alive; °חַיִּין (pl.) life, חייכון by your life!; חֵיוַת בָּרָה see בר.

חיט (< חטט) *pa.* to perforate.

חַיִל, חַייל strength, suff. °חַיְלֵהּ.

חֵימָה anger (H.).

חכם to know; חכם sage, scholar (H.); °חַכִּים wise.

°חָלָ sand.

חֶלְבּוֹן Helbon (place name).

°חַלָּה casket (cf. J. T. Milik, in *Revue Biblique*, LXV [1958], 409).

חִלָּה valley.

חלל *ap̄.* to desecrate.

חלם *etp.* to gather strength, to recover.

חֵלֶם, חֵילֶם, °חֲלֵם dream.

חלף see לחף.

חולף in the place of, instead of.

חלפו, חֶלְפְּתָא (proper names, cf. Mishna Ms. Kaufmann).

חוּלָק (= חֲוּלָק?), °חוּלָק, °חֲלָק (= *ḥᵒlaq*) portion, share.

חמד (*pᵊʿal* and *pa.*) to desire, to covet.

חמה to see; *etp.* to pretend.

חֲמוֹר Hamor.

°חֲמָר donkey, חַמָּר donkey driver.

חֲמַר wine.

°חֲמֵשׁ, חַמְשָׁה five; °חַמְשִׁין fifty.

°חֶן grace, favor; °חַנָּן merciful; חנינה, חנניה (proper names).

חנק to choke.

חַס lettuce.

°חֲסֵד, °חֶסֵד kindness, grace; חַסִּיד pious.

חסן *etp.* to settle; *ap̄.* to inherit; *ettap̄.* to acquire possessions.

חַסִּיר wanting, minus, empty.

חֲקַל, °חֲקֶל (f.) field.

(חר) בַּר חוֹרִין free man.

חרב, חריב to be ruined, destroyed; *etp.* to be destroyed; *ap̄.* to destroy.

°חֲרֶב, חֶרֶב (f.) sword, det. °חַרְבָּה.

חוּרְמָן venomous (snake).

חורן see אחרן.

חרץ loins, det. חַרְצָה, pl. suff. °חַרְצֵיךְ.

חרקנוש (proper name).

°חָרָשׁ, f. °חָרָשָׁה sorcerer, sorceress.

חשב *pa.* to sum up.

חִתָּאָה Hittite.

*חֲתוֹרָה breach, opening (made by digging), det. °חֲתוֹרְתָה.

ט

°טָב, f. טָבָה good, (pl. f.) °טָבָתָה goods, טָב לְ– better for, טָב קַרְתָּה representative of the city; טָבָאוּת well, properly. See also טוב.

טַבְלָה °some part of a floor mosaic (?) (Latin *tabula*).

טבריה, טיברייה Tiberias.

טִיבּוּר umbilical cord (vocalization as in Mishna Ms. Kaufmann).

טוּב goodness, טוּבָךְ blessed!

טוף to drip, to be inundated.

טוּר mountain, det. °טַוְרָה (!), pl. det. °טַוְרַיָּה (!), cstr. °טוּרֵי (!).

טוש to smear.

טיכסה wall (Greek τεῖχος).

טִימִי (f.) payment, value (Greek τιμή).

טַל dew.

טְלֵי young man, det. °טַלְיָה.

טמי (< עַטְמֵי, cstr. of עַטְמִין) bones.

טמע to set (sun).

טמר *pa.* to hide.

טעה to be lost.

טען to carry.

טפה to extinguish.

טפטה carpet, pl. טפטין (Greek τάπης, -ητος).

י

°יֶבֶידָה lost object.

יְבוּל growth, produce.

°יְגַר heap of stones.

°יַד, °אִיד, °אֶיד (f.) hand; לְיַד, לְיֵיד to, at the side of.

ידה *aph*. to admit, to acknowledge, to confess, to praise.

ידע to know.

יהב to give, יהבון להון "let them have it!", יהב ונסב to deal. Cf. נתן.

יְהוּדָה Judah, Judaea.

יְהוּדָאי, יְהוּדָי, יְהוּדָיי Jew.

יְהוֹנָתָן Jonathan.

יְהוֹשֻׁעַ Joshua.

יוֹאָב Job.

יוּדָן (< יְהוּדָה) (proper name).

יוֹחַי (proper name).

יוֹחָנָן Johanan.

יוי abbreviation of the Tetragrammaton.

יוֹם° day, יוֹמָה דֵּן, יוֹמָה הָדֵין today, בָּתַר יוֹמִין after a while, מִן יוֹמוֹי ever, at all. See also ימם.

יוֹנָה (? יַוְנָה°) Jonah.

יַוְנֵי (יבנה, cf. גו) Jabneh (place name).

יוֹנָתָן Jonathan.

יוֹסֵה, יוֹסֵי (< יוֹסֵף) proper name.

יוֹסֵף Joseph.

יוֹעֶזֶר Joezer.

יוש׳ = Joshua.

יכח *aph*. to admonish, to reprove.

יכֵל to be able.

יְלֵד (*pᵉʿal* and *aph*.) to give birth.

ילף see אלף.

ים sea, det. יֶמָּה°, יַמָּה, pl. יַמְמִין.

(ימם, אִימַם°) באימממא by day.

יַמִּין° right, right hand.

יסף *aph*. to add; *ettaph*. to be added.

יַעֲקוֹב Jacob.

יִצְחָק Isaac.

יקד *aph*. to set on fire, to burn; יְקִידָה°, יְקֵידָה° conflagration.

יְקָר°, אִיקָר° honor.

יַרְדְּנָא Jordan.

ירושלם Jerusalem.

יְרַח moon, month.

יְרֵת to inherit, to take possession of; יְרוּתָּה heirloom.

יִשָּׂשכָר Issachar.

יִשְׂרָאֵל Israel.

יִשְׁמָעֵל (= ישמעאל) Ishmael.

יָת° accusative particle.

יְתֵב° to sit, to dwell; יְתִיב°, יַתִּיב° sitting.

יַתִּיר excessive.

יְתַם orphan, pl. יֶתְמִין°.

יתוש gnat, mosquito.

כ

כ like as (conj.), like (prep.), הא כ- see היך. See also כמה, כמן.

כבש *pa*. to subdue.

כַּד°, כְּדֵיי° when, as.

כַּדּוּ (< כד הוא), כַּדּוּן° now (cf. G. Dalman, *Grammatik*, 2nd ed,. 102ε).

כדב *etpa.* to be insincere.

כְּדֵן see דן, גין.

כָּה here.

כָּהִן priest; כְּהוּנָּה priesthood.

כָּהֲנָא (proper name).

°כָּוְויָה (= כַּוְיָה ?) burn.

כוך sepulchral chamber, det. כּוּכָּה (?, cf. כּוּכִים in Mishna Ms. Kaufmann).

-ד° כֵּיוַן (-כֵּיוָן ד ?) since, as soon as.

כְּוָת see ות.

כּוּתָאי Samaritan, pl. כּוּתָאֵי.

כַּחֲדָא see חד.

כָּךְ thus, so.

כֹּל, כּוֹל all, entire, every, everyone; כל די whichever, דְּהִיא . . . כֹּל whatever it may be; כְּלוּם something, anything, (with negation) nothing.

כלל *pa.* to crown (sing for, dance around) a bridal couple on its wedding day.

כְּמָה, כְּמָן how many ?, how much ?, however much (many); -כמה ד (conj.) just as.

כמן to lie in wait, to hide.

°כֵּן, כֵּין thus, so, כן וכן so and so; בְּכֵין then, thereafter.

כְּנַעַן Canaan.

כנש to gather; *etpa.* to gather (intrans.), to be gathered; כִּנְשָׁה gathering of people, crowd, congregation, כְּנֵישְׁתָה synagogue, בכנישתה see בי.

כסי *pa.* to cover; כְּסוּ (f.) clothing.

כְּסַף, °כֶּסֶף, °כְּסֵף, °כְּסֶף silver, money.

°כְּעַן now.

°כַּף (f.) palm of the hand, hand.

כִּיפְלָה double amount; כָּפֵילָה double.

כָּפֵילְתָּא (place name).

כְּפַר חִיטַּיָּה (place name).

כרך *pa.* to wind around, to wrap.

כְּרַם, °כְּרֶם, °כֶּרֶם vineyard.

בֵּית כַּרְמָא Beth Hak-kerem.

כשבה see בר.

כשר to be proper, fit, right.

כְּשׁוּר beam.

כתב to write, to write down (expenses); °כְּתָב writing, letter, ledger.

כתת *pa.* to pound, to crush.

ל

ל to, for, accusative particle, °with (instrumental).

°לָא no, not. See also הלא.

לֵאָה Leah.

לבדין clothes made of felt.

לָבָן Laban.

לִבְנָן Lebanon.

לְבֵשׁ to put on (garment); *ap̄.* to clothe in; °לְבוּשׁ garment.

להוד see הוד.

לוט to curse.

לוֹט Lot.

לֵוִי Levi.

לויה, לוויה caravan.

לוּלַב palm branch, pl. לוּלַבִּין.

לְוָת see ות.

לחוד see חד.

לחף *šap̄.* שלחף (< שחלף) to change.

לֵילֵי night, det. °לֵילְיָה.

לִיעֶזֶר (< אֱלִיעֶזֶר) proper name.

לית lion, det. לֵיתָה.

°לֵית, °לֵית there is not (none), not.

°לְמָה why? See also דלמה.

לֵסְטָאי robber, pl. לֵסְטָאֵי (Greek ληστής).

לעה to work, to study; °לְעוּ (f.) labor.

לְעֵילָא, מִלְעֵילָא above.

לקט *pa.* to pick, to gather.

לקיש proper name.

לְרַע (< לארע), מִלְּרַע below.

לִישָׁן, °לֵישָׁן, °לְשָׁן (cf. H.) tongue, לִישָׁן בִּישׁ evil talk, denunciation.

מ

מ- see מה, מן.

°מְאָה hundred, pl. °מָאוָון; ◇מאתיך your two hundred (?) (read מאתין [?] two hundred?).

מֵאכַל food.

°מָאן vessel, garment.

°מַבּוּלָה, °מַבּוּלָה the flood.

מַבּוּעַ well, spring.

מגד fine fruit, pl. מִגְדָּנִין.

מגר *pa.* to overthrow.

מַדְבַּח altar.

מַדְבַּר desert, det. °מַדְבַּרָה(!).

מְדוֹר dwelling.

מְדִינָה, מְדִנָה, מְדִינָה country, city, det. מְדִנְתָּה, ◇מדיתה.

°מַדְנַח east.

°מָה, מ- what?; מה, מהא (interjection) what is the matter!; °מָה דְּיי whatever. See also כמה, למה.

מְהֵימָן see הימן.

מוֹעֵד festival.

מוֹת death.

מותב see בי.

מוֹתַר remainder.

מזג to mix, to temper.

מזגה (place name).

מְזוּזָה door-post.

מוֹחַ brain, head.

מחה to hit, to smite; מַחָה stroke.

מָחוֹז harbor, city (Akk.).

◇מחזרו (f.) return.

◇מחניה (f.) camp (H. ?).

מחצלה mat.

מטה to arrive, to reach; *ap̄.* to bring.

מטכסה silk (Greek μέταξα).

מַטְמוֹעַ sunset (cf. *Tarbiz*, XXII [1950–51], 56 [offprint, 20]).

מְטַר° rain.

מַטְּרָה guard, service, post.

מי see מן.

מֵילָה wool (Greek μηλωτή).

מֵימַר word.

מימנתי see הימן.

מַיִן° water, det. מַיָּיה°, suff. מוי.

מֵין see מן.

מינוק, מיינוק, מנוק child, boy.

מית to die; מִית dead; מִיתוּ death. See also מוֹת.

מכך *ap̄.* to lower; מַכִּיךְ low.

מְלָא fullness. See also מלי.

מַלְאַךְ° angel.

מִלָּה word, thing, pl. מֶלִּין°, מִלִּין, suff. מִלֵּיכוֹן°.

מְלַח salt.

מלי *pa.* to fill; מְלֵי full.

מֶלֶךְ king; מַלְכוּ (f.) kingdom, government.

מַלְכִּצֶדֶק Melchizedek.

מלל *pa.* to speak. See also מִלָּה.

מָמוֹן° money, wealth.

מַמְרֵה Mamre (proper name). See also אלוני.

מַמְרֵי Mamre (place name).

מִן, מֶן°, מֵין°, מי־, מ־ from, because of, than, (מן ד־) belonging to, מן ד־ as soon as, after (conj.), (מן with part.) while (cf. *Tarbiz*, XXII [1950–51], 190ff. [offprint, 33ff.]).

מַן° who?, מַן דִּי he who.

מנה to count; מִנְיָן° count, number.

מְנַחֵם Menahem.

מנן see אן.

מנוק see מינוק.

מְנַשֶּׁה Manasseh.

מְנָתָה (det.) share, portion, עַל מְנָת even at the risk of.

מס tribute, tax, det. מִסִּין.

מסבלה (proper name).

מסטובי, מיסטובי stone bench (< Greek στοά?).

מִסְכֵּן poor man.

מסר to hand over.

מַעֲמַק depth, pl. מַעֲמַקִּין.

מַעֲרַב west.

מְעָרָה cave.

מפקה expenses, (charitable) contributions.

מַצּוּ quarrel.

מִצְוָה, מִיצְוָה religious command, meritorious deed, pl. det. מֶצְוָתָה°.

מִצְרַי, מִצְרָיי Egyptian; מִצְרַיִן Egypt.

מקדון Macedonian (Μακεδών).

מקדש temple. See also בי.

מקור beak.

°מְקָמָה objects, goods.

מר see אמר, מרה.

מרד to rebel.

°מרדיע saddle-cloth.

מָרֵה, מָרֵי lord, master, suff. מָרִי, etc.

מרצע borer, awl, det. °מַרְצְעָה.

מרר *etpa.* to quarrel, to fight.

°מֶרְתוֹק (ת!) fist.

משׂבלה (שׂ!) (proper name).

מֹשֶׁה Moses.

°מְשַׁח oil; מְשִׁיחָה Messiah.

מִשְׁכַּב bed, grave. See also בי.

מַשְׁכּוֹן, מישכון security, pledge.

°מַשְׁרְי, °מֶשְׁ[רִי] camp, resting place.

מִשְׁתֵּה drink.

מתל parable, pl. °מיתלין.

מַתְנַן (place name = Bashan).

נ

נבי prophet, det. נְבִיָּה; נְבִיו prophecy.

נגד to flow, to travel, to draw; *etp.* to stretch oneself, to die.

נגע *ap̄.* to reach, to come into contact with.

נגריה see אנגריה.

נדד to flee (sleep).

נְהַר river, det. °נַהֲרָה.

נוח to rest, to lie.

נוּר fire, light.

נַחוּם (proper name).

נָחוֹר Nahor.

נְחַל brook.

נחמן (proper name).

נְחָשׁ copper.

נחת to go down, to come down.

נטל to move, to travel.

נטר *pa.* to guard.

נְכַס, נְכֵס to slaughter; נִכְסָה slaughtering.

נכס (pl. נִכְסִין) property.

°נִימוֹס law, usage (Greek νόμος).

נֵיס miraculous event, pl. (—ין) נִיסִים.

נְסֵב, נְסַב to take, נְסֵיב אַפִּין to favor, נסב איתה to marry, נְסִיב אִיתָּה married, *ap̄.* to give in marriage. See also יהב.

נסה to take.

נסה *pa.* to try, to test.

נִיסֵּיתָה (place name = Massah).

נעו wine press, vat, det. נַעֲוָה.

נפח to blow, to breathe, תפח רוחיה, let him go to Hell!

נפל to fall, to lie down (impf. יִפֵּל).

נפק to go out, נָפֵק וְעָלֵל coming and going; *ap̄.* to take out, to bring out, to spend, to dismiss.

נַפְשׁ, °נפֶשׁ, נֶפֶשׁ (f.) soul, life, עַל נַפְשֵׁיה for himself.

נַפְתָּלִי Naphtali.

נצב to plant.

נצה *etp.* to quarrel.

נצח to be victorious; נִצְחָן strength, victory.

נצל *aῡ*. to take away.

נקם to take revenge on, to be hostile to.

נשׂי prince (title,) det. נְשִׂיָּה.

נשה *etp.* to forget.

נשין see אִתָּה.

נתן to give (impf., inf.; cf. יהב).

ס

סאב *pa.* to soil, to defile.

סָב elder, old man, ancestor.

סְבַע satiated.

°סבק (= שבק) to leave, to leave behind.

סבר to believe, to understand; *pa.* to hope, to trust; *aῡ*. to explain.

סגה (שׂגוּ; *(sᵊgî* Gen. 49:22) to grow, to thrive; *aῡ*. to increase, to make much; °סְגִי, סַגִּיא numerous, large, great, °סִיגִּין, °סְגִין, סַגִּי exceedingly, greatly, very much (cf. G. Dalman, *Grammatik*, 2nd ed., 102ε).

סגר to close, to lock.

סודם Sodom.

°סְדַר study, prayer (cf. Theodor-Albeck, 689), order (of laws); °סְדָר hall of study, synagogue (cf. H. Yalon, *Quntrēsīm*, II, Jerusalem 1938–39, 4 n. 6; L. Ginzberg, *Yerushalmi Fragments*, I [New York 1909], 82, l. 37).

°סָהֵיד witness. See also שָׂהֵיד.

סוסי horse, pl. סוּסָוָן.

°סוֹף end.

יַם סוּף (a body of water).

סחה to swim, to bathe.

סחר to go around, to travel; *aῡ*. to surround; סְחוֹר סְחוֹר all around.

*סטו stone bench, det. °סטוה (Greek στοά) (cf. J. N. Epstein, in *Tarbiz*, I [1929–30], 152).

°סִימָה treasure.

סִינַי Sinai.

סייע *pa.* to aid, to assist; °סִיעָה group, band, party.

סְיָף end.

סכה °to think (?); *pa.* to wait, to hope, to look out.

סַכִּין knife.

סלע (f.) a coin, det. סִלְעָה.

סְלֵיק to go up; *pa.* to remove; *aῡ*. אסק to bring up, to lift, to bring.

סמך *etp.* to lean.

סמק to be red. See also שׂמוּק.

סָנֵא enemy.

סְעֵד, סְעֵיד support, assistance.

סֵעִיר Seir.

סְפִינָה ship.

סָפַר scribe, teacher; **סֵפֶר חַיִּים** Book of Life (H.).

סְפָר border, border district, **סְפָר יַמָּה** seashore.

°סְקוֹל, **°סְקוּל** mishap.

סרב *pa.* to decline, to refuse.

סתו winter, det. **סִיתְוָוה**.

סתר secret, det. **סִתְרָה**.

ע

עבד to do, to make, to produce, to act, to labor (impf. **יעבֵד**); **עבדת גרמה** she pretended to, **מה ... עֲבִיד** how is he ?; *etp.* to become; *pa.* to produce; *šap̄.* to subdue; **°עֲבֶד** slave, servant; **°עוֹבָד** (= **עֲוֹבָד**), **°עֲבָד** (!) fact, case, work, activity.

(**עבע**) **°לעובע** quickly (cf. E. Y. Kutscher, *The Language of the Genesis Apocryphon*, in *Scripta Hierosolymitana*, IV [1957], 8, 11).

עֲבוּר, **עֲבוֹר** grain.

עבר to pass (**ב־** by), to cross; *pa.* to become pregnant, **°מְעַבְּרָה** pregnant.

°עִבְרָאִי °עֶבְרָיי Hebrew.

עַד until, to (prep.), **עַד דִּי**, **עַד ד־**, **עַד** until (conj.).

עֲדַב lot, share, det. **עַדְבָּה**.

עדה to pass by, to cease.

עִדָּן time, period.

°עֲדֵר, **°עֲדַר** flock, det. **עֶדְרָה**.

עוק *ap̄.* to press, to annoy, to distress. See also **עָקָה**.

עולה see **בר**.

עור *etp.* to bestir oneself, to awake.

עֵז see **ענז**.

עוּזִּיָּה Uzziah.

עילא see **לעילא**.

עיין, **עין** eye (det. **°עַיְנָה**), (pl. **עֵיָנוון**) spring, well; **כְּעֵין** like, similar to.

עַל upon, about, above, to, for, against, in addition to, according to; **עַל ד־** because, since (conj.); **עַל אַפֵּי** before, in front of; **עִילָוֵי**, **°עֲלָוֵי** on, upon.

עלל to enter; *ap̄.* to cause to enter, to bring in. See also **נפק**.

עֲלָלָה harvest, corn.

°עָלַם, det. **עָלְמָה** world, eternity, **חַיֵּי עָלְמָה** (life in) the other world, **לָא ... לְעָלַם** never, **מִן עָלְמָה** from eternity, **עַד עָלְמָה** until eternity.

עוֹלֵימוּ (= **עֲלֵימוּ**) (f.) youth.

עַלְעוּל whirlwind.

עִם, **°עֶם** (together) with.

°עַם people, nation, pl. **עַמְמִין**.

°עַמּוּד column.

עמק valley.

°עמר to heap up, to gather in the field and bring into the house.

°עומרה dwelling, house.

°עָן, °עָאן small cattle.

ענה to answer.

(ענז) עֵז goat.

עֲנִי poor, det. עַנְיָה.

עֲנָן, °עֶנָן cloud.

עסק to take pains, trouble, עסיק ב־ occupied with.

עֲסַר ten; תְּרֵי עֲסַר twelve.

עֲפַר dust.

עפרון Ephron.

°עֵיצָה counsel (H.).

עָקָה worry, distress, suff. °עָקְתְהוֹן.

עקר to uproot; *pa.* to mutilate, to hamstring (horses).

ערב *etpa.* to be mixed, to intermarry.

עַרְבָה bough of the willow tree, pl. עַרְבִין.

ערובה eve of the Sabbath, Friday.

קִרְיַת ערביה (place name).

עורביי Arab.

°עָרְלָה prepuce.

ערנם (proper name).

ערס bed, det. עַרְסָה.

ערע *pa.* to meet, to happen to; °לעורעה toward him (cf. Syriac *lura'*).

ערק to flee.

עֵשָׂו Esau.

°עַשְׂרָה ten; °עֶשְׂרִין twenty. See also עסר.

עַתִּיר rich.

פ

פגל radish, det. פּוּגְלָה.

פגע to meet (ב־ someone).

פדע wound, det. °פָּדְעָה (= פַּדְעָה ?).

פייס *pa.* to persuade, to pacify, to conciliate (< Greek πεῖσαι).

פלג to divide, פְּלִיג differing in opinion; *pa.* to distribute; פֶּלֶג half; בְּעֵל פַּלְגוּ adversary.

פלח to work, to serve; פָּלַח worker, servant.

פלט to escape.

פלטאנוס (name of a place, near Sichem).

פִּילִי gate (Greek πύλη).

פְּלָן so-and-so.

פילקי prison (Greek φυλακή).

פְּלִשְׁתָּאֵי Philistines.

°פֶּם, °פֵּים (°פֵּם, °פֵּים) mouth (the form °פום appears to be a copyist's error under the influence of Eastern Aram., cf. *Tarbiz*, XXI [1949–50], 203 [offprint, 14]).

פונדקיי innkeeper (Greek πανδοκεῖον).

*פני evening, det. פַּנְיָה.

פניים (place name).

פסיפס mosaic (Greek ψῆφος).

פסק to cut, to cease.

°פעל property (?) (cf. Theodor-Albeck, 784).

פצה to save.

פק in בפקי end (of the Sabbath).

פקד *pa.* to command, to exhort, to appoint as executor.

פקע to burst.

°פֵּירִין (pl.) fruit.

פרגמטווט tradesman, merchant (Greek πραγματευτής).

°פּוּרְדֵּס garden, park (cf. Greek Φορδησων, see J. T. Milik, in *Biblica*, LXVIII [1961], 77 ff.).

°פאריטין servant, sexton (?) (Greek ὑπηρέτης ?) (= אפריטון = חזן ?, cf. J. B. Frey, *Corpus Inscript. Iud.*, I, p. XCIX).

פרן *pa.* °to take as a wife by paying the bride price; °פְּרֶן, °פְּרֶין, פרני bridal gift, dowry (< Greek φέρνη).

פָּארָן Paran.

פַּרְנָס community leader, administrator (of charity donations) (Greek πρόνοος ?, cf. S. Fraenkel, *Die aram. Fremdwörter* [Leiden 1886], 280, but see C. Brockelmann, *Lexicon Syriacum*, 2nd ed., 599a).

פּוּרְעָנוּ punishment, retribution.

פורפירה purple cloth, royal garment (Greek πορφύριον).

פרק to unload, to deliver; פִּרְקַת צור neck; פֻּרְקָן salvation.

פרש to set aside, to distinguish; *pa.* to separate, to disclose.

פָּרָשׁ horseman.

°פורת Euphrates (cf. E. Y. Kutscher, *The Language of the Genesis Apocryphon*, in *Scripta Hierosolymitana*, IV [1957], 24).

פשט to stretch out.

פִּתְגָם word, thing.

פתה to be wide; *ap̄.* to widen; פְּתָי, פותי width; פְּתֵי, (f.) פַּתְיָה wide.

פתח to open, to begin.

פתי see אפתי.

פתן serpent, det. פִּתְנָה.

צ

צִבְחַד (often misspelt צבחר) a little.

צְבַע dye, color, (pl. צִבְעָנִין) dyed clothes.

צִיבּוּר congregation, crowd.

°צַדִּיק just, virtuous, pious.

צוח to shout, to call; *pa.* to shout, to cry, to complain.

צור neck, det. צַוְּרָה.

צִידוֹן Sidon.

צלי *pa.* to pray; °צְלוֹ (f.) prayer, blessing.

צמת *pa.* to gather (trans.).

צְנִין cold (vocalized in L. Ginzberg, *Yerushalmi Fragments* [New York 1909], 170, l. 5).

צער *pa.* to grieve; צְעַר pain, grief.

°צפה to look.

צַפִּיתָה (place name = Mizpah, Gen. 31:49).

צִיפּוֹרִין (place name).

צְפַר morning, לְצַפְרָא the next morning.

צְרִיךְ needing, (he) must.

ק

קָאֵם, קָאֵים (root קום) followed by another participle to indicate durative action (corresponding to Eastern Aram. קא).

קבל to complain; *pa.* to accept, to receive; לְקֳבֵיל toward.

קבר to bury; קְבוּרָה grave, burial.

קְדָל back of the head, neck.

קדם *pa., ap̄.* to precede, to anticipate, to come to meet; °קְדָם, °קֳדָם, קֳדָם, °קוֹדָם, קומי, קמי before (prep.), מן קדם before, from (before), לית קומיך you do not have; (קְדָם) מִלְּקַדְמִין from of old; קַדְמַי first, °בְּקַדְמָיְתָה, בְּקַדְמֵיתָה in former times.

קדש (place name).

קַדִּישׁ holy, holy one; קוֹדֶשׁ holiness; °לָשָׁן בֵּית קָדְשָׁה the Hebrew language; °קִדּוּשִׁין (pl.) a wife's additional settlement beyond the usual one (?).

°קְהָל congregation, crowd.

קום to stand, to rise, to stop (part. קָאֵים, קָיוּם); *pa.* to establish, to fulfil, to keep alive; *ap̄.* to put, to place, to erect, to appoint; קיים alive. See also קָאֵם.

*קוץ thorn, pl. °קוֹצִנִין.

קור crane (cf. Theodor-Albeck, 712).

קטל to kill; *pa.* to kill; קטל, det. קַטְלָה killing, capital punishment; קְטוֹל slaying; קְטִיל corpse (of an animal).

קטסטיס settled order, settlement (Greek κατάστασις).

קטע to cut.

קטר to tie, to harness.

קְטוֹרֶת incense.

°קילוון, °קילייון I have ordered (< Greek ἐκέλευον) (cf. S. Lieberman, *Greek in Jewish Palestine* [New York 1942], 8).

°קְיָם (f.) covenant, oath.

°קָיְימָה (°קָיֵימָה) pillar.

קֵיסְרִין Caesarea.

°קָל voice.

קלל *ap̄*. to behave disrespectfully toward.

קלס *pa*. to do honor (by singing, dancing) (< Greek καλῶς).

קלק *pa*. to throw.

קָמָה standing grain.

קמי, **קומי** see **קדם**.

קמץ (palm of the) hand, det. **קוּמְצָה**.

קִנְיָן property.

קנס to punish, to fine (< Latin *census*).

קסט a liquid measure.

קפד meat, piece of meat (Greek κοπάδιον).

°קפאדוקיה, **°קפדוקיה**, **°קפדוקייא** Cappadocia.

קפח *pa*. to rob.

***קצי**, f. **°קצייה** (most) remote (**מלכו קצייה**, referring to the kingdom of the ἔσχατοι ἀνδρῶν, cf. S. Lieberman, *apud* B. Mandelbaum, *Pesikta de Rav Kahana*, 474).

קיקלה dunghill, det. **קִיקִילְתָּה**.

°קיקן plough, det. **קִיקְנָה** (cf. Syriac and *Aruch Completum*, VIII, Suppl., 74).

קרא, **קרה** to read, to call, to name, to crow; **קרא** Bible verse.

קרב to approach; *pa*. to bring near, to offer (sacrifices); **°קוּרְבָן**, **קָרְבָן**, **°קוֹרְבָּן**, **°קָרְבָּן** sacrifice, forbidden (as a **קורבן** is to a layman).

קְרָב war.

קְרֵי(?), **קריה**(?), **קרייה**(?) city, village, det. **קַרְתָּה**, suff. **°קַרְתֵּהּ**, pl. **קְרֵי**(?), det. **קריה**, **קרייה**, suff. **°קְרְיֵכוֹן**, cf. T. Nöldeke, *Beiträge zur semitischen Sprachwissenschaft* [Straßburg 1904], 61, and *Neue Beiträge* [Straßburg 1910], 131 n. 5. The situation in Galilean Aram. is not clear).

קרע to tear up.

קירוש frost, det. **קֵירוֹשָׁה**.

קְשֵׁי, f. **°קַשְׁיָה** hard, difficult.

ר

ר׳ = **רבי**.

רְאוּבֵן Reuben.

רֵאשׁ, **רֵישׁ** head, chief, beginning, **רֵישׁ שַׁתָּה** beginning of the year.

°רַב great, elder, senior, teacher, pl. **רַבְרְבִין**, **°רַבְרַבִין**(!), **רַבְרְבָנִין**, pl. det. also **°רביה**; **°רַבִּים**, **°רֶבִּים**, **רִבִּים** Rabbi (title of scholars) (for the vocalization, see Mishna mss. and transliterations, cf. E. Y. Kutscher, *The Language and Linguistic Background of the Isaiah Scroll*, 48); **רַבֵּינוּ** (= **רבנו**) our teacher, title of Rabbi Judah Han-Nāśī (H.);

°רַבּוּן, °רַבּוֹן, °רִבּוֹן lord, master (cf. NT ῥαββουνει, — ωνει, see *Zeitschrift für die Neutestamentliche Wissenschaft*, LI [1960], 53; *Henoch Yalon Jubilee Volume* [Jerusalem 1963], 268).

רִבּוֹ myriad, pl. רִבְּוָן, det. רִבְּוָתָא.

רבי *pa.* to raise, to anoint.

רָבִי girl.

רבע to lie.

רִבְקָה Rebecca.

רגג *šap.* to entice.

רְגַז, רְגֵז anger, det. רוּגְזָה, suff. °רוּגְזִי.

רְגַל, רֶגֶל (f.) foot, leg, suff. רַגְלוֹי; רִגְלָאי foot soldier, pl. רִגְלָאִין.

רדה to plough.

רדף to pursue.

°רוּחַ (f.) wind, soul, quarter (four directions). See also נפח.

רוּם height, majesty. See also רָם.

רוֹמִי Rome (for the vocalization, cf. Mishna Ms. Kaufmann); רומיי Roman.

רָז secret.

רָחֵל Rachel.

רחם to love, to have pity; °רַחְמָן merciful, compassionate.

רוּחְצָן safety, לְרוּחְצָן safely.

רחק *pa.* part. pass. מרחק abominable.

°רֵיקָן empty.

רֵישׁ see רֵאשׁ.

רָכֵב rider.

°רכס roof, ceiling (cf. F. Schulthess, *Lexicon Syropalaestinum*, [Berlin 1903], 194b).

°רָם high; רָמָה height. See also רוּם.

רמה to throw, to put, to throw oneself (upon someone).

רמי (*pa.*) to deceive (ב– someone); רמאי, f. רַמָּיָה deceiver; רַמָּיו fraud, deceit.

רמון (place name).

רְמַשׁ evening, det. °רָמְשָׁה (*romšā*).

רע see לרע.

רעי to desire, to want, to welcome, הֲוָא רְעִי ב– he liked (the girl); רְעוּ wish, pleasure; °רַעֲוָה pleasure.

רָעֵי shepherd, pl. cstr. °רעה (!).

רפה *ap̄.* to leave alone.

רקד *pa.* to dance.

רְתַךְ chariot, pl. רְתִכִּין.

שׂ

שׂגה, שׂגי see סגה.

°שָׂהֵד, °שָׂהֵיד witness, f. שָׂהְדָה; °שָׂהֲדוּ testimony. See also סָהֵיד.

שׂחק to laugh.

°שִׂים situated.

°שְׂמָאל, שְׂמָל left, °north, suff. °שַׂמָּאלֵיהּ (= שַׂמ׳, °שְׂמָ׳?).

שְׁמוֹק red. See also סמק.

שׂנא see סנא.

שְׂנִיר Senir (mountain).

שָׂרָה, שָׂרַי Sarah.

שׁ

שְׁאֵל° to ask, (בִּשְׁלָם) שְׁאֵל to greet.

שאר *eṯp.* to remain; שְׁאָר° remainder.

שַׁבָּה, שׁוּבָּה° Sabbath, week.

שֵׁבֶט tribe.

שבי to capture, to carry off; שבי captivity, det. שִׁבְיָה; שביה captives, booty, det. שְׁבִיתָה.

שְׁבִיל path.

שְׁבַע seven.

שבע *eṯp.* to swear; שְׁבוּעָה°, שְׁבְעָה° oath.

שֶׁבַע בֶּן בִּכְרִי (proper name).

שבק to leave, to let go, to reduce (מינהון their number).

שגח *ap̄.* to mind, to care (ב־ about).

שַׁדַּי Shadday.

שדך *pa.* to calm, to pacify.

שדל *pa.* to persuade.

שדר *pa.* to send.

שהה to tarry.

שוא (Valley of) Shaveh.

שוי *pa.* to place, to set, to make alike, to make, to saddle; שִׁיוָי couch; שוה immediately (cf. S. Lieberman, *Greek in Jewish Palestine*, 176f.; *Leshonenu*, XXV [1961], 125).

שוק street, market, det. שׁוֹקָה°.

שׁוּר wall.

שׁוֹר see שר.

שֵׁיד demon, det. שֵׁידָה.

שיצי to finish, to exterminate.

שכב *ap̄.* to put down (a sleeper, a corpse).

שכח *eṯp.* to be found; *ap̄.* to find, to be able.

שְׁכֶם Shechem.

שְׁכִינָה divine presence, Shekina.

שכר *pa.* to make drunk.

שלה° to cease.

שלח *pa.* to send; שְׁלִיחַ messenger.

שלחף see לחף.

שׁוּלְטָן rulership, power, office, ruler, governor, suff. שָׁלְטָנוֹי; שִׁלְטוֹן, שִׁילְטוֹן ruler, governor; שַׁלִּיט° powerful, ruler.

שְׁלִם to be peaceful, to be friendly; *pa.* to pay, to recompense; שְׁלָם° peace, הֲוֵה שְׁלָם farewell (at the end of letters), הֲוָה לִשְׁלָם to live peacefully; שְׁלִים perfect; שָׁלֵם Salem (= Jerusalem); שָׁלוֹם (H.). See also שאל.

שֵׁם°, שום (שׁוֹם) name, pl. שְׁמָהָן, מן שמי in my name.

שְׁמוּאֵל Samuel.

°שְׁמַיָּא, °שומיא heaven (cf. E. Y. Kutscher, *The Language and Linguistic Background of the Isaiah Scroll*, 392).

שמע to hear, to listen to, to obey; *etp.* to obey.

שִׁמְעוֹן Simeon.

שמרון (name of a demon).

שָׁמְרָיי Samaritan.

שמש *pa.* to wait upon, to have sexual intercourse.

שמש sun, det. °שִׁמְשָׁה, שֶׁמְשָׁה.

°שֵׁן, °שֵׁין tooth.

שנה *pa.*, *ap̄.* to change.

שנה sleep, suff. °שֶׁנְתִּי.

שְׁנָה year, det. שַׁתָּה, pl. °שְׁנִין.

שָׁעָה hour, time.

שעבד see עבד.

שפי *pa.* to compensate (inf. °משופיה, cf. E. Y. Kutscher, *op. cit.*, 391).

שפע *ap̄.* to pour out, to give in abundance.

שפר to be pleasing; °שָׁפַר beauty, cf. also בַּי.

שקי *ap̄.* to give to drink.

שׁוֹר umbilical cord.

שרה to loosen, to untie, to unharness, to dwell, to rest, to encamp; *pa.* שרי, °שוריי to begin (cf. E. Y. Kutscher, *op. cit.*, 392 n. 244); שֵׁירוּי beginning.

שרב heat of the sun, dry heat, det. °שַׁרְבָה.

°שַׁרְבִיט staff, stick.

שרגג see רגג.

שרע to slip, to fall.

°שֵׁת six, שִׁתָּה, det. שיתי (cf. G. Dalman, *Grammatik*, 2nd ed., 129).

אשתי, אישתי to drink.

שתל to plant.

ת

תבע to search, to inquire, to demand; °תָּבוֹעַ אדם blood revenger.

תבר to break, to injure, to rout.

תגר *etpa.* to trade.

°תְּהוֹם the deep.

תוב to return, to go back; *ap̄.* to bring back, to give back; תובן again.

°תּוֹר ox, תּוֹרָה cow.

תּוֹתָבוּ settlement, (temporary) residence.

תְּחוּם, °תְּחֻם border, limit, district.

°תְּחוֹת underneath (prep.).

תכל *pa.* to be childless, to make childless.

תַּלְמִיד pupil, student.

תְּלָת, °תְּלָתָה three; תְּלִיתָיי third; תְּלָתֵּהוֹן the three of them.

תם see התם.

תּוּמַיָּה see אוריה.

תמה *ap̄.* to be astonished; תְּמִיהַ wondering.

°תַּמָּן there.

תְּמָנְיָאת עֲשַׂר eighteen.

תנה *pa.* to report.

תנחום (proper name).

*תניה (?) beam, det. °תניתה, °תנייתה.

תִּנְיָן, °תִּנְיָין second; °תִּנְיָנוּת a second time.

תיסווריה, תיסוורייה (pl.) treasury (Greek θησαυρός).

תעל fox, det. תַּעְלָה.

תַּפְנוּק delicacy.

תקל to weigh.

תקן *pa.* to prepare, to set in order, to make things legally fit for use (by giving the priests and Levites their due).

תְּקֵף to be(come) strong, powerful; *pa.* to strengthen; תְּקוֹף, תּוּקְפָּה power, strength; °תַּקִּיף strong, mighty, protector.

תרא see תרע.

תרד beet, pl. תּוֹרְדִין (in Latin transliteration *thoreth*, cf. E. Y. Kutscher, *The Language and Linguistic Background of the Isaiah Scroll*, 392 n. 244).

°תְּרֵין, °תְּרַיין, תְּרֵי, °תר, (f.) °תַּרְתֵּין, °תַּרְתַּיין two (cf. G. Dalman, *Grammatik*, 2nd ed., 125); תְּרֵי עֲסַר twelve; °תְּרֵיהוֹן, תַּרְתֵּיהוֹן both of them.

תַּרְנְגוֹל rooster.

תרך *pa.* to drive out.

תרע *pa.* to break, to make a breach.

°תְּרַע door, gate, det. תַּרְעָה, °תרא.

תַּשְׁלוּם payment, in payment for, pl. cstr. °תַּשְׁלוֹמֵי, °תַּשְׁלוּמֵי.